ALL ABALONE

ARE DEAF

BY

FELIX MACIAS, JR.

ILLUSTRATIONS BY
PEGGY FONTENOT

Revised and updated
for Second Edition

Typesetting, design and editing by
Platt & Company
P.O. Box 908
Gualala, California 95445
phone (707) 884-4707
email: wendy@plattcompany.com

TABLE OF CONTENTS

ACKNOWLEDGEMENT

This is the Second Edition of my book. I have been working to improve the book for many reasons: in order to save all abalone, teach other people to respect abalone and their resources, to help the future of the businesses all over the North Coast and for my friends.

Before I started writing this book, I went out abalone diving many times only for a catch of the day. I usually got one or two, just enough for dinner because I like to eat fresh abalone. Before I say anything, I would like to thank everyone who helped me get this book finished. First of all, I would like to make a list of dedications to...

To the memory of Harry Lester Hauschildt, 1954-1995, my first abalone dive buddy. Hey, Harry, remember our old days when we first rockpicked with our clothes, not wetsuits in real thick fog in very early morning at Fort Ross in about 1979. I can't remember if we got any, but it sure froze me and I swore that if I came back, it would be with wetsuits.

To the memory of my friend, John Darby, 1942-1998, known to us as Abaloneman, my chief competitor of abalone cooking and my favorite dive buddy. Hey Abaloneman, remember our old days, when we went out abalone hunting

Andrea kissing her proud dad, Felix with his first catch of abalone in 1988 before his first day of his new job at Salt Point State Park.

and spearfishing at the Fort Ross Reef. Diving with you was the hardest working day I ever experienced in my entire life. I never want to do that again. The challenge really wore me out because we had to make some trips down and up the cliff with our dive gear, scuba gear, tanks weighing about 50 pounds each plus 30 pounds weightbelts!

We stayed in water for almost half day just to look for a big abalone, hunting for big fishes and to enjoy the very calm ocean. I even took a nap on the divefloat while you still hunted!! When we were done with our diving, we brought our limits of very big abalone and many fish: 2 big 25+ pound lingcods, 2-20+ pound cabezos, 3 huge red snappers and several rock fish for a total of over 100 pounds.

We were excited with our catches, but for me, I kept thinking of the cliffs that I had to climb while hauling these catches, the gear, and our belts back to our truck. Two more trips up and down the cliffs to haul!! At the end of the day, I was so tired but you kept cleaning, fileting, cooking a dinner for us and yet, you still danced and celebrated. I swore that if I ever do that again, I had better be in very good shape.

To the craziest, diehard divers, Silver Seal (Ralph Singleton) and Red Snapper (Tom Drabek). If it wasn't for those two guys, I may never have any fun or any crazy dives. One now became the first deaf certificated scuba instructor and the other is now in the Marshall Islands. Last I heard, he may be back soon to the USA in search of a lady.

To my two ladies, Karan and Andrea, for being patient with me all through my book. Andrea, thanks for correcting my language. If it wasn't for you, I may be not have finished this book.

To all the locals of the North Coast (from Fort Ross to Stewarts Point), for being my friends.

The Three Abalone Amigos, Ralph Singleton, Felix (the author) and Tom Drabek with their first proud catches of clicker abalone in 1989 with my help. See how proud they were!

ABOUT THE AUTHOR

AND HIS LIFE ON THE COAST

It's only 3 hours from the Bay Area to get here, so how can I convince my friends to come visit me? That was my first reaction after moving here from the Bay Area after I got promoted from my first state job at Half Moon Bay State Beach. First of all, I have to introduce myself to you all and tell you why I decided to make this book.

My name is Felix Macias Jr. and you may wonder why this book is called All *Abalone Are Deaf*. Well, I am deaf and **all abalone have ear-shaped shells**. Just take a good look at the shell and you will see the earshape. What's more, deaf people can talk with sign language underwater with anyone, anything, and of course, abalone.

I also want to be sure that you clearly understand the rules, safety precautions, and most of all, the *abalone*. For 10 years I have seen drownings around here because people do not follow or listen to the rules or safety precautions. I have also seen people get arrested for abalone-related illegal activities like undersizes, overlimits, transporting abalone out of shell, and poaching.

I moved to California in 1977 with my friends who live in the Bay Area after dropping out of Gallaudet College in Washington D.C. I met Karan and have been with her for 20 years now. I have a 14 year old daughter, Andrea who goes to Point Arena High School. I was born and raised in East Chicago, Indiana, working four summers with the City Parks of East Chicago. That's how I started getting interested in working for the parks.

I worked in a small park with many winos and bums hanging around. There was so much broken glass and bottles all over that I had to make friends with them. They started to have respect for me and their park and helped clean up it up. That's what I wanted...to have people respect me, their parks and its resources.

I got my first California state job with Half Moon Bay State Beach in 1983 and continued working there until 1988. I got promoted to Salt Point State Park and moved into state-owned house with my family, Karan and Andrea who was 4 years old at the time. Naturally, I was very nervous and had culture shock because I had never lived in the woods and didn't know if my friends would ever visit me. There was no good T.V. reception around here at that time, no one who knew sign language, and my closest neighbors were deers, racoons and skunks which was a bit spooky as I had lived in a city all my life.

I was a basketball and softball player and coach for all deaf teams, went to deaf clubs and social places in Bay Area, Who would want to coach a team with deer, skunks and racoons? A lonely place for me, a deaf guy alone on the North Coast, but I was glad that I brought my family here with me. I was thinking, how can I get my friends to come here for a visit?

I went to my neighbor. Not the skunks or deer, but a Hawaiian guy who also works with me, and asked him to teach me how to dive for the abalone. He took me out. Splash, he went in the water so quickly, like a seal, that I had to chase him. I swam very hard. Afterwards, I realized that I was not that good a swimmer and not in very good shape...I blamed it on too much booze. He could stay in the water for a long, long time like a whale. He popped up on the surface with a big, white teethy smile and showed me a big abalone he caught down below. I was little tired and little scared because I never been in the water before. But I caught a first abalone 10-incher...my first fish story. To be a fisherman or abalone diver, you have to tell *little* lies. All right, I caught a clicker abalone but was so proud of it. I think I still have that first shell somewhere along my fence.

I brought that first abalone to the Bay Area just to show and tell and cook for my friends. I cooked them the best fried abalone fry and gave them all tastes. They asked me where I had gotten them. I told them to come up to visit and dive with me. A big, tall man with a fat beard came up to visit me saying with a loud, seal-barking sound voice, in big sign language "Show me my abalone!" Behind him an eager young man wearing two hearing aids and a very old worn-out rental wetsuit was waiting for his first dive.

First we went out rockpicking on very good low tide, and didn't get any good-sized abalone, but at least we got the limit. We had a great time, and they came a little more often. The next time they came with the better gear, better, bigger boats and better skills.

But, I was happy with the new people I met and ate with at the campgrounds all over the coast. I started asking for recipes and saved them for this book. I have cooked and eaten all of the abalone recipes in the book.

One day a rusty-faced man with red, salty hair came to me at one of the campgrounds, and introduced himself, saying "My name's Cap' Ab" in broken sign language and wanted to introduce me to his lady. I was expecting a real lady, but instead he showed me his beloved red-painted boat. No wonder, his name is Cap' Ab, well-known on the coast because of his knowledge of good places to fish and get good abalone. Remember that I am **deaf** and **don't read the lips very well.** Later, that day I was working on the truck when an Abalone Ranger in a full brown and green uniform wearing a neat Smoky Bear hat came from out of nowhere and said a quick "hello." He looked over me, saying "I can smell something funny." Suddenly he disappeared so fast, I didn't even have a chance to shake his hand. I knew he was going to some big action somewhere!

Beware of the Abalone Ranger
He can feel you,
He knows what you doing
He watches you
From anywhere, behind the rock,
Up the tree, in the ocean
Watching you all the time!
Beware of the Abalone Ranger!

That's a **big warning** to all poachers who have broken the Department of Fish and Game rules for divers!!! He will watch you all the time because I have seen him in action many times.

When I first came, I started at Salt Point State Park which has 5,970 acres, and is 20 miles north of Jenner on Highway 1. There are two campgrounds, Gerstle Cove and Woodside, a sandy beach, Stump

Beach, a Visitor Center and an underwater reserve for divers and Kruse Rhododendron State Reserve which contains 317 acres of beautiful second-growth redwoods, Douglas fir, tan oak, and of course, rhododendrons. I stayed there for almost eight years.

I now work at Fort Ross Historic State Park, an historic fort built by Russians in 1812 as an outpost for sea otter hunters and a permanent trade base. There is a Russian Orthodox chapel and three other reconstructed Russian buildings, and a Visitor Center with exhibits, and Fort Ross Reef Campground.

One day I was working at the shop, when two Russian Rangers, a tall one with a neat trimmed mustache and another short one with real long hair and short beard, dressed up in Russian Military uniforms for Living History Day, (held on last Saturday of July), came in and greeted me together in Russian, roughly translated, "Welcome to Fort Ross." They always work together, greeting all people in Russian and they are true Fort Ross Russian Rangers!

On the way home, I stopped by a small old store built in 1860 with a nice dive camp to buy a drink. A man with a neatly combed Italian hairstyle and a clean trimmed "Admiral"-type beard was smoking a cigar behind the counter and said to me "What's up out in the ocean?" He had listened to many fish stories because I had noticed the people from dive camp stopped by to tell their many fish stories, mostly about the big ones they caught that got away. He told me that he caught some big fish, at first I didn't believe him because he had plenty fish stories he got from other people. Then I noticed he had some pictures to prove it. Remember, a picture with a big fish or abalone is worth a thousand words (and can't tell a lie).

There always are locals sitting on the deck in front of the store, greeting people as they drive by. We became friends and buddies, and I joined them sitting on the deck.

I went up north to check on my mail at the old post office. On the way I noticed a big eagle soaring high above the redwoods on the hill, then flying over the ocean, back to the hill, I know there's a spirit watching her people all over the coast.

There is an old post office and a very old general store built in 1868, and a tall, sturdy man with long rolled mustache and ocean wave hair, walking away from his 1929 Model A car, saying "Well, my car's very old. So is my store. So I am not going to get old!" No wonder he has lived here all his life, as do his parents, and grandparents. They're the locals sitting on the porch, waving at us, too.

Later in the evening, I went up on the hill and looked at the ocean, saying "What a beautiful sight with a fish hawk carrying a fish, a herd of deer running into the bushes, and a mermaid out there lying on a rock at Salt Point with wavy, brown hair, abalone-colored eyes dressed in a kelp bathing suit with a half moon in the sky." Out on the ocean were lots of whale spouts all over as they migrated north. I love the ocean so much that I promise to give back to the ocean by writing this book to help save the abalone and make sure our children and grandchildren will have abalone in their future.

WHAT IS AN ABALONE AND ITS HISTORY?

What is an **ABALONE**? "A sea mollusk with an oval, somewhat special shell," as described in **Webster's New World Dictionary**. A "mollusk" is a group of invertebrates that includes oysters, snails, squids, etc, and is characterized by a soft body, often enclosed in a shell.

Abalone are one of the most sought-after shellfish, or "gastropods." They have only one shell compared to other mollusks, like clams or oysters, that have two shells. The soft body is a muscle that is attached to the shell. The "foot," called a mantle, attaches the abalone to its resting place. Black circular fringe with tentacles, the *epipodeum*, surrounds the foot. Two eyestalks, similar to a familiar garden snail, are called "myopic eyes."

Abalone are well-known for their incredible strength in clinging to rocks. Huge suction cups, helped by water displacement and protected by a massive shield of shell, make abalone almost invulnerable from being wounded or injured during an attack.

When used as food, a legal-sized abalone makes at least a quarter pound of meat. Extremely large red abalone can yield as much as three pounds.

Abalone eat marine algae. The adults feed on loose pieces that drift with surge or the current. Large brown algae such as giant kelp, feather boa kelp, and elk kelp are preferred. Abalone tend to stay in one place waiting for food to drift by, but they do move daily or when food gets scarce for extended periods. Scuba divers at night have seen abalone climbing a stalk of giant kelp to feed on the algae. The color on the shells is often due to the types of algae eaten. For example, red abalone eat red algae.

Abalone have their own predators that eat them: starfish, octopus, crabs, sea otters, fish (cabezons can swallow a whole abalone!) and man.

Determining the age on abalone is difficult as abalone shells have no marks for deciding how old they are. The juvenile abalone grows an inch or more per year for the first two years. Red abalone mature at 1.5" to 2.0" per year but the growth process slows with age. A seven inch red abalone (a legal-sized catch) may be 7 to 10 years old. The largest recorded size of a red abalone was almost 12-1/2" in length! A "ten-inch abalone" is uncommon, but if caught, it is considered a big prize or a trophy for the abalone diver. In ten years of working along the Sonoma coast, I have seen only about a dozen of them.

There are eight species of abalone along the Pacific coast, although some scientists believe there are only seven. The most common are red, pink, green, white and black. The common *red abalone,* is found from Oregon to Baja California; the *black abalone,* from Mendocino County to southern Baja California; the *green abalone,* from Point Conception to Bahia Magdalena in Baja California; the *pink abalone,* from Point Conception to Santa Maria Bay in Baja California including Channel Islands; the *white abalone,* from Point Conception to Bahia Tortugas in Baja California, and the Channel Islands. The other less common abalone are the *flat abalone,* found from British Columbia in Canada to San Diego, California; the *pinto abalone,* from Sitka, Alaska to Monterey, California; and the extremely rare *threaded abalone,* from San Luis Obispo County, California to Bahia Tortugas, Baja California. The pinto abalone is called *northern abalone* at commercial fisheries in Alaska and Canada.

Abalone can be found on the Pacific coast on rocky intertidal and subtidal areas from Alaska to Baja California. Red abalone may be found in cold northern California waters from south Oregon to Baja California. Abalone seek cover in crevices and under rocks to protect from predators. They are active at night while they move around to find food. Abalone can be found from low tides to more than 50 feet deep. In the remote areas, abalone can be found in abundance in very shallow water. Many abalone find homes hanging upside down in shallow cracks. Productive abalone areas often have a thick layer of palm kelp growing off the bottom.

Abalone have been along the Pacific coast of North America for millions of years and scientists have found fossilized shells similar to the abalone that are about 100 million years old. For centuries, the native Indians of California have used abalone for food, tools and decorations (jewels).

Why Northern California has so many abalone makes me wonder. During early 1800s, Russian settlers came to the western coast of North America at Fort Ross to hunt sea otters for fur. Abalone are the sea otter's favorite food. The sea otters were hunted almost to extinction. After the otters were gone, abalone population increased along the coast.

Biologists have determined that there are three reasons why the abalone population is so healthy in the northern part of the state and so poor in the south: In Northern California there is no commercial take and scuba diving for abalone is not permitted, plus there are no sea otters. The commercial harvest of abalone, not legal on the northern California coast, started in the early 1930s on the southern California coast. It grew to seven million pounds by 1970.

Sea urchins compete with abalone for food. Commercial urchin divers currently harvest millions of pounds of urchins a year, clearing more food for abalone. Some commercial urchin divers also have commercial abalone licenses which they use to poach by harvesting abalone from the north coast, then taking them to the south coast, claiming the abalone were caught off Farralon Island or elsewhere on the south coast.

The abalone population on the south coast has been diminishing due to disease, resource mismanagement and over-harvesting, a result of legal tank usage. Effective in 1998, a ban on taking abalone on the south coast has been implemented.

Up on the north coast, poaching is the biggest problem, a result of the black market where abalone can be sold for anywhere from $50 to $100 per pound. This causes poachers to take more than their limit and undersized abalone. The Department of Fish and Game estimates that up to 25% of abalone harvested on the north coast was taken illegally.

Divers need to be careful while hunting for abalone as abalone blood does not clot well. If an abalone is injured by an improperly used abalone bar, it dies. Coastal development and pollution have ruined many areas of abalone habitat.

There are private organizations working to save abalone by preventing poaching, promoting better management of abalone population, offering lectures on how to catch abalone properly and developing new rules.

Abalone divers and rock pickers must have an abalone stamp and a fishing license. As of 1999, a Resident Sport Fishing license is $27.05. To legally take abalone, an additional $12.00 stamp is put on the license.

A few divers have complained about the new "tax," however many divers, as myself, do not! We don't complain as the stamp will help insure that our children and grandchildren will have abalone in the future.

The new stamp is a step in the right direction. The research funded by the stamp will heighten our abalone management skills and improve the abalone population. Better ways to stop poaching are now spreading all over the coast. You can help by reporting poaching, taking only your limit and know the fishing rules and regulations. Please help by teaching your friends how to respect them. Let's follow the rules; take only what we intend to eat, and ensure that there will be abalone for all, FOREVER!

Top of the abalone: just caught off Ocean Cove.
See the color; red with growth of kelp and barnacles on it.

Bottom of the abalone: has black circular fringe
with tentacles called the epipodeum, *and the foot called the* mantle.

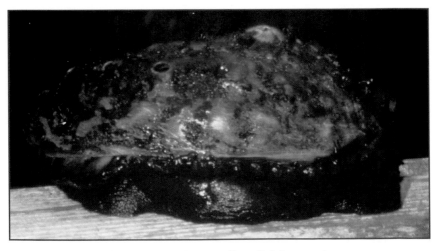

Side of the abalone: has eyestalks called the myopic eyes,
with kelp still attached to the shell.

Note the Mother of Pearl color under the abalone shell.
That is what all people are attracted to. It is most commonly used
for jewelry, soap holders and even for landscape decorations.

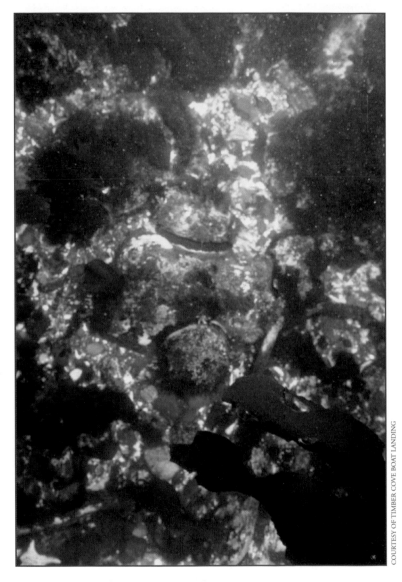

Imagine yourself in the ocean looking for abalone.
How many abalone do you see in this picture?

CALIFORNIA SPORT FISHING REGULATIONS

You are required to obtain a fishing license in order to get any fish, and dive for any abalone. It is the law that must be followed to avoid any fines.* **The law now provides for a minimum $250 fine for fishing without license.** You can purchase a license at any bait shop, and sporting goods store. The cost is dependent on the type of fishing. There are fishing licenses for saltwater, fresh water or both. Beginning January 1, 1998, the **abalone stamp** is required for taking abalone and must be attached to your sportfishing license. The cost of the stamp is $12.00. Funds will be used to enforce, educate, conduct research and manage the abalone habitat.

There is quite a bit of misinformation about abalone regulations among newcomers to the sport of abalone diving *and* the veterans. I will give you a quick reference on the Rules and Regulations in plain language after the actual statements from Rules and Regulations.

POSSESSION AND DISPLAY OF LICENSE

Section 700 (Title 14, California Code of Regulations).

(a) *Display of Sport Fishing License*: Every person while engaged in taking any fish, amphibian or reptile, shall display their valid sport fishing license by attaching it to their outer clothing at or above the waistline.

Persons diving from a boat or shore may have their license on the boat or within 500 yards of shore.

Means: **You have to show your license above your pantline up on your clothes while fishing from a boat** or shore at all times. For divers, if you dive from a boat, you must have a license on the boat. If you dive from the shore, you must have a license within 500 yards of the shore.

Anyone *16 years and older* must have a fishing license to take any kind of fish, mollusk (abalone), invertebrate, amphibian and crustacean.

29.05.General:

(d) In all ocean waters skin and SCUBA divers may take invertebrates as provided in this article except that in all ocean waters north of Yankee Point (Monterey County), self-contained underwater breathing apparatus (SCUBA) may used only to take sea urchins, rock scallops and crabs if the genus Cancer.

> *Means:* You *can't* use scuba gear to take abalone north of Yankee Point. *Snorkeling gear for free diving* and *rockpicking from rocks on shore* are allowed along the North Coast. In other words, you must hold your breath.

29.10.General:

(a) Saltwater mollusks can be taken only on *hook and line* or with the *hands*.

(b) The size of a mollusk is measured in greatest shell diameter.

> *Means:* **You can take any mollusks by fishing lines with hooks or by your hands. Measure the shell at its greatest size for the legal size.**

29.15.Abalone:

(a) *Limit:* From North of Yankee Point, in Monterey County, four in combination of all species, except that no black, pink, green, or white abalone may be taken or possessed. Minimum size measured in greatest shell diameter. Red abalone, seven inches. All legal size abalone detached must be retained, and a person shall stop detaching abalone when the bag limit is reached.

> *Means:* You can take RED ABALONE from North of Yankee Point, in Monterey County. You can never take more than FOUR (4) per day of legal size abalone. Even if you dive for a few days, you must not have more than four abalone on you at all times. Undersized should be put back to the same place immediately. NO HIGH GRADING - You must *stop* after taking four legal sized abalone. You can't exchange the small legal-sized abalone for a bigger one after taking limits. NO DRY SACKING - Everyone must take their own abalone. You can't give the abalone to other persons at any time.

(b) *Open season:* North of Yankee Point (Monterey County) abalone may taken only during the months of April, May, June, August, September, October and November.

> *Means:* You can take abalone in the months of April to November, except the month of July. The month of July is breeding time for abalone.

(c) *Fishing hour:* One-half hour before sunrise to one-half hour after sunset only.

> *Means:* You can't take any abalone from 1/2 hour after sunset to 1/2 hour before sunrise.

(d) *Abalone retained:* No undersized abalone may be brought ashore or aboard any boat, kept on the person. Abalone not retained must be replaced immediately with the shell outward to the surface of the rock from which detained. Abalone not attached in the shell may not be transported or possessed, except when being prepared for immediate consumption.

Means: You can not take any undersized abalone any-where at any time. When you bring an undersized abalone to the surface the of ocean after a dive, you must put it back in the same place where you found it. Abalone without shells are not allowed to be brought home or anywhere, unless they are to be eaten right away. *To avoid a fine, NEVER transport an abalone without it being attached to the shell.*

(e) *Special gear provisions:* Abalone may taken by hand or by the devices commonly known as abalone irons. Abalone irons must be less than 36 inches long, straight or with a curve having a radius of not less than 18 inches and must not be less than 3/4 inch wide nor less than 1/16 inch thick. All edges must be rounded and free of sharp edges. Knives, screwdrivers and sharp instruments are prohibited.

Means: You can take abalone with your hands or an abalone iron. Irons must be less than 36" long, not less than 3/4" wide or less than 1/16" thick. No screwdrivers, knives, or illegal bars are allowed be-cause if the abalone is cut in any way, it will bleed to death. Remember: abalone are hemophiliacs which means that their blood does not clot well. *Absolutely* NO SHARP EDGES!

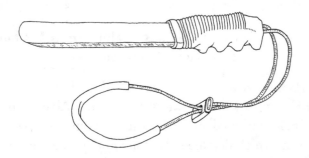

Abalone iron: Note there are no sharp edges.

(f)*Measuring Device:* Every person while taking abalone shall carry a fixed caliper measuring gauge for accurately measuring the species of abalone being taken. The measuring device shall have a fixed opposing measuring arms which are of sufficient length to allow abalone to be measured by placing the gauge over the shell of the abalone.

Means: All persons *must* have *at all times* while diving for abalone, their own measuring device or a fixed caliper gauge that shows 7" between two arms. It is a *violation* to take abalone without a gauge, even if the abalone taken are not undersize.

Fixed caliper measuring gauge for abalone

Sport caught abalone **may not** be sold for commercial purposes. Abalone or abalone parts (i.e., shells, pearls, etc.) taken under sportfishing license may **not** be sold for any purposes.

Means: You *can't* sell any abalone, shells, pearls or anything connected to abalone at any time.

Anyone convicted of a violation involving abalone, is subject to a fine of five times the market value of the abalone taken or ten thousand dollars, whichever is greater, imprisonment in county jail for up to a year, loss of their license for up to 10 years, or a combination of all these penalties.

Means: You can get a fine for possessing undersized, over limit, transporting an abalone without the shell, selling abalone on the black market, taking an abalone out of season or any crime connected to an abalone. They may take your diving gear, boat, vehicle, and you may spend time in jail...ZERO TOLERANCE! Last time I heard the fine is about $350 per abalone each for all violations.

If you see or hear of someone taking abalone illegally, call the CalTip hotline, 24 hours a day, seven days a week. Even if you remain anonymous, you may be eligible for a cash reward.

1-888-DFG-CALTIP or 1-888-334-2258

SAFETY TIPS FOR
ABALONE DIVING

The Sonoma and Mendocino Coast provides divers with some of the most beautiful and unique sea life in the world. The steep coastline caused by the large swells from storms, 2,000-3,000 miles away, can cause some very rough conditions. The swells, "sleeper" waves (two sets of waves doubling up to form one huge wave), rip currents, longshore ocean currents and the rough coastline can make the unwary divers' experience unpleasant. Remember that ocean conditions can change drastically in a matter of hours.

Diving is a very strenuous sport and you must be in good shape before diving. Check your gear to make sure it is in good condition, then check the water. **Your life** may depend on this decision. I have seen some drownings around here because of unfortunate accidents. This is why I have written tips to help save divers.

The spring season makes some of largest tide changes, highest surf, poorest visibility, and rough weather for the beginning of the abalone season. The fall season often gives the best conditions, but always be prepared for changes in ocean and weather conditions.

What makes abalone diving so challenging? Try slipping into a wetsuit on a drizzly, foggy morning on the north coast. Once suited up, slip into the frigid, murky waters to search for prey. Sometimes, become the prey. To make a safe dive, abalone divers need good equipment, good physical stamina, mental attentiveness, a good dive partner and good ocean conditions. There are no crowds to cheer for you, no scorekeepers!

New divers should go for a minus tide for a dive. Experienced divers prefer moderate tides and deeper waters. New divers, if lucky, will take the first legal abs they see. Experienced divers will go for larger abs. Most agree that "ten-inchers" are not that easily discovered...Here are eight tips for abalone divers, down below!

(1) **Buddy** – Always dive with a BUDDY, no matter how good you are in freediving or rockpicking. You could get overtired, have trouble swimming back to shore, or get caught in the kelp, and have no one around to help you out. One buddy should stay on the surface while other dives. That way they can watch and help each other. Let me repeat again, ALWAYS DIVE WITH A BUDDY!

(2) **Exercise** – Do exercises and get in good shape before going out for dives. This is one of most important tips of all. Do not overestimate yourself if you have had little or no exercise. You will find out how hard it is on the first dive if you are **not** in good shape! Walking, running, swimming, are all good preparation for diving.

(3) **Water Condition** – Always study the ocean conditions before you get in the ocean. Know where the safe entries and exits are in case of emergencies. Ocean conditions can change in matter of minutes. Do not force yourself if the condition is not good.

(4) **Peer Pressure** – Do not overestimate yourself. Know your limits. If you are inexperienced, dive with a more experienced diver. Do not force yourself if you do not feel right or feel not well. Do not give way to peer pressure!

(5) **Health** – Sleep, rest, good preparation will give you the BEST abalone dive. Long drives, alcohol, drugs, and smoking cigarettes are a nightmares for **all** abalone divers. **Healthy divers are happy, alive abalone divers with four big abalone!**

(6) **Equipment** – Always check your gear before you go into water. *Wetsuit* – try it on before you drive to the coast as you might be surprised to find you gained some weight (or muscle). *Weight belt* – check that the right weights are on the belt and the release buckle works. *Mask and snorkel* – make sure they fit you well and are in good condition. All the equipment should be checked and tried on at home before driving to the coast.

(7) **Surface Support** – Abfloat, tube, mat or any floating device can give you a place to rest while on the surface, store the abalone that you've taken while looking for more, plus help you carry gear to and from the shore, up and down the hills. They can save your life, too.

(8) **Know the Ocean Rules and Regulations** – Please read all rules and regulations before you go on abalone dives. That way you will help the abalone population and keep them for the next generation. You will not be worried about being caught doing illegal activities and can enjoy yourself!

BE SAFE AND RESPECT THE OCEAN…IT'S MOTHER NATURE!

HOW TO PICK AN ABALONE

It is very important to know how to properly pick an abalone. Abalone are hemophiliacs, which means their blood fails to clot normally, causing prolonged bleeding from even minor injuries. The Department of Fish and Game have made studies that show that even with extreme care, abalone are cut at least 12% of the time when pried off a rock. If the abalone is wounded, it will bleed to death or be easy prey for predators attracted by the blood from their injuries. If the abalone is undersized and must be replaced, it probably will die. When you replace an undersized abalone, be sure it is firmly clamped down. *Extreme care* must be taken to avoid cutting abalone when removing it. The best practice is to pick only *legal size* abalone. Remember: things may be appear to be 25% larger underwater than on the land.

You will need a proper *abalone iron* and a proper *abalone gauge*. Abalone iron must be regulated to minimize the chance of cutting the abalone. It must be smooth without any sharp edges. Follow the Department of Fish and Games Rules and Regulations for the exact information, as described in the book in the chapter entitled California Sport Fishing Regulations, **29.15.Abalone (e)Special gear provisions.** and **29.15.Abalone (f)Measuring Device.**

Remember: Absolutely NO SHARP EDGES!

The proper way to "pop" abalone from the rock is to slide the iron between the foot and the rock, then lift the handle up. Do not push on the handle in a way that forces the iron into the foot. If you happen to see an abalone in the open, you can just grab the shell quickly before it clamps down to the rock without using the iron.

After taking your limit, if you happen to see a 10" abalone on way back, you are not allowed to put one back and take the larger one in its place. That is called **High Grading** and is not allowed under the sport fishing regulations. Everyone must take their own abalone and are not allowed to give abalone to another person with a license who has not dived. That is called **Dry Sacking** and is also illegal.

The proper way of removing an abalone.

How to Clean, Prepare, Tenderize and Store Abalone

Cleaning an **ABALONE** is a really disgusting and messy job, but if you really want to eat or taste the abalone, you have to clean it first. The most important of tools is a proper abalone iron and a very good, sharp filet knife that will help you cut, and not waste any meat.

It is important that the abalone be shucked when fresh. Abalone will keep in the refrigerator for a few days but will lose about a half cup of its milk which will cause it to lose a good deal of the delicate flavor unique to abalone. If you are not going to use the entire muscle right away, freeze it immediately after shucking. The unwanted portions (darker pieces) can be trimmed after the abalone thaws. One of the most common mistakes in cleaning the abalone is the attempt to salvage too much meat.

Naturally, prepare for the big mess.

The first step is to clean the abalone.

1) Put the abalone, shell down, on any hard surface. Hold the abalone and put the iron between the shell and the meat at the front, the pointed end of the shell.

2) Push gently toward the center of the shell to separate the meat out of the shell. This may take some force to try to pop the muscle loose. Be careful not to break the shell. Always keep the iron in contact with the shell, so as not to waste any meat. You may have some problems at first.

3) Once the meat is free from the shell, pull or separate the membrane from the edge of the shell. Pull the gut from the meat. Put the guts in a bag to be discarded properly **OR** save them for fish bait.

4) Wash the abalone thoroughly to remove sand or other debris that will dull your knife.

5) Using a sharp knife, cut the intestines from the meat and the tough skin from top to bottom.

6) Cut the top of the abalone where it attached to the shell.

7) Cut a deep "V" shaped wedge to remove the mouth.

8) Trim off the epipodeum (the black tentacled edges around the abalone). Try not to cut too much as you can wash it off with a good scrubber.

9) Trim the very thin brown skin off from the bottom of the abalone. Again, try not to over trim, just get the brown skin.

10) Wash the abalone off very well.

The second step is to prepare the abalone.

Depending on the recipe you use and whether you plan to cook or store the abalone, there are different ways to prepare the abalone.

• It can be cooked as a whole.

• It can be sliced with hands or an electric meat slicer. Using an electric slicer is great if you have one, however, if you don't, follow these instructions. Place the whole abalone on a hard surface. I prefer using a cutting board. While holding it firmly, start slicing 1/8 to 1/4 inch thick horizontal pieces. **OR** break a wooden coat hanger in half and nail it in the shape of a "V" to a board. Wedge the abalone into the "V" and start slicing.

• It can be ground through the meat grinder, preferably a strong grinder as the abalone is tough.

• It can be cut into cubes.

Remember, abalone should be cooked quickly. If cooked too long, it becomes tough and chewy.

The third step is to tenderize the abalone.

There are several different ways to tenderize the abalone as the meat is very tough unless tenderized. Here are several options:

• *This is my way of tenderizing the abalone.* First pound a whole abalone a few times with an ab pounder (a meat tenderizing mallet), then cut slices about 1/4" thick, but not less than 1/4". Pound the slice a few times on each side and it will be delicate and soft.

• Hold the whole abalone firmly with one hand and pound it with a flat smooth ab pounder few times on both sides all over the abalone.

• Wrap the whole abalone in the center of a towel and place it on any hard surface. Strike it with mallet or 2x4 piece of lumber a few times **OR** sling the towel-wrapped abalone onto a hard surface a few times.

• Grind the meat through the meat grinder will soft the meat.

The last step is to store the abalone.

There are different ways to store the abalone. *Remember: only if the abalone is ready to be consumed, can you take it off the shell.* It should be cooked immediately. To avoid a fine from the California Department of Fish and Game, according to the Rules and Regulations, *never* transport the abalone without the shell.

You can store the live abalone in an ice chest for up to a couple of days until you are ready to clean them. *Abalone Tip: to bring them home alive* – put your abalone on the inside side of the chest as they will cling to the wall with their heads upward (the holes are the head end). Ice them down and leave the drain open so water won't pool inside. The ice lowers their metabolism and as long as they don't get the fresh water, they will sort of hibernate all the way home.

To freeze the whole abalone with the shell, store it in a freezer-strength ziplock bag with a little water, remove as much air as possible, and put it in the freezer until you are ready to clean and eat it. Most people will clean the abalone and store it in a freezer bag with a little water without the shell then put it in a freezer, as this tends to save space. *However, remember, that storing the abalone without the shell may be seen as a violation.*

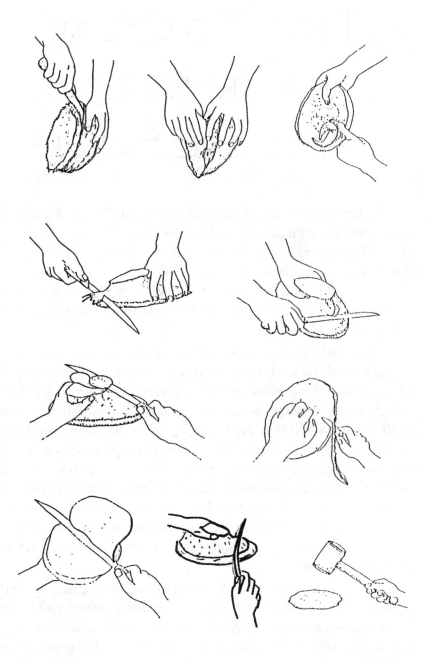

Removing an abalone from its shell, trimming, slicing and pounding an abalone.

How To Clean and Prepare an Abalone Shell

"**Ahh, Ohh, What a beauty of abalone shell!**" is a big compliment that I always recieve from the people when I show them abalone shells. The beauty of the abalone shell, inside and outside, is what people most admire, want to keep and take it home. A main reason of why the shell is truly admired is the color of mother of pearl inside and an attractive red exterior when it is done with cleaning, scrubbing, and preparing.

There are different ways to clean and prepare depending on the conditions of the shell. Before you start cleaning and preparing, always use **breathing mask, eyewear protection** such as a **goggles** or **safeglasses**, and **rubber gloves**. The fine dust from scrubbing the shell is **VERY POISONOUS and DANGEROUS**. It can be hazardous to your lungs and your health. The acid or lye can burn your skin so be sure to wear all safety gear at all times. Work with a partner, wear the safety glasses, mask, and work outside or in an open-ventilated area with a bucket of water or a garden water hose nearby in case of an emergency. Keep children, pets and valuable things away from the work area. **Let me say again, always wear mask, safety glasses and gloves all the times.**

You have to be a fussy with your selection of the condition of the shell. Choose the shell with little or no growth, no chips, and healthy surface, also with few or no pitholes on the outside and beauty of the inside. Place the shells at the corner of the backyard to get some sunlight for several days. After the shell is dry, scrub it with a wire brush real well, of course, wearing a breathing mask. Remove the stubborn growth or barnacles with a small chisel. Place shell inside down and cover well with water. Pour with 3-4 tablespoons of lye granules and soak for 4 to 24 hours. Rinse well with water from a garden water hose. Once again, scrub the outside with the wire brush and inside with steel wool pad. Muriatic acid may be used carefully to remove the stubborn growth and stains. Too much acid can destroy the delicate shell. Put a small amount of the acid to the area that needs a deep clean for about 30 seconds. Be careful with that acid, wear all safety gear: glasses, mask and goggles. Rinse the shell with lots of water, too, after using the acid. Dry the shell very well and coat it with mineral oil tp preserve its shine.

There are different ways to keep the shell lustrous and shiny. The first is the paraffin way which I learned from someone else. Warm the oven to 200 degrees. Melt 1/4 cup of wax in a small can. Brush wax all over the shell. Put the shell in the oven with the newspaper under to catch the dripping wax until the wax is melted. Remove the shell and wipe off the excess wax with a paper towel.

The second way is to coat the shell with mineral oil or linseed oil. The luster will last longer if you plan to display the shell indoors. Of course coat it once a while, too. Resins, shellacs, and varnishes are fine, but can turn yellow and crack with age and not are natural to the shell.

Then the last thing you do with the shell is to **ADMIRE AND SHOW IT OFF!!**

THE LARGEST ABALONE

John Pepper with his huge abalone shell, measuring 12 5/16" length and 9 3/4" width. Courtesy of Ocean Cove Store and Campground.

LARGEST!!! BIGGEST!!! HUGEST!!! MONSTER!!! are the favorite common terms that everybody especially the divers talk and brag about their abalone all the time at the campgrounds. Hey, it is not very easy for us, the divers, to find any BIG abalone around here in the present time. What we are talking about is that a big **10"**, a ten-inch abalone is a true **TROPHY** or a **PRIZE!**

Many veterans keep telling me that they used to locate them in large sizes with ease years ago. What I am talking about now is that the Department of Fish and Game Marine Laboratory takes serious action in recording the sizes of the abalone now. Ever since the dept. started sport records of all abalone lengths, the last document was the top ten red abalone that were recorded since 1983, and they all were all brought from the locations north of Fort Bragg.

A diver named John Pepper of Montara, California had the largest abalone ever recorded with its length of **12.3 inches (12 5/16")** with **9 3/4"** in other length, weight of **11 1/2** pounds with from both shell and meat, and the shell itself that was weighed **5** pounds and **1 1/2** ounces! It was caught off the Humboldt County coast on September 5, 1993 at 5 pm. Of course, John won't disclose an exact location of where he found it. A foot-long abalone is not common! It is still not easy to get that size. John plunged about 12 feet down and saw the abalone wedged back about four feet out of the wall of the cliff. After two hours of hardworking, prying and scraping with his abalone bar and surfacing every 55-60 seconds for more air., he finally brought in that **GODZILLA OF ALL ABALONE!!**

Everyone in the diving and marine biology communities was really amazed with its large size. The divers in general have pride in their trophies or prizes just because they have either better diving skills, better scuba gear, better technology, knowledge of safety and better floating devices such as a kayak or a zodiac. Some divers have been searching for the largest abalone for a long time and tend to reject small ones. Some just get their limits so they can feed their families and friends. They want to improve their fish storytelling, and mostly, have FUN.

I have seen about a half-dozen ten-inch long abalone all along the coast. I mean a real live abalone in my 10 years. Every time I see such a huge abalone, my eyes pop out, my jaw with my tongue out falls to the ground saying, "**Oh my gosh, Son of Abalone!**" Plenty of meat to cook for sure, but you have to know how old the abalone is. Each abalone must be over 15-20 years old. John Pepper's abalone might be about over 40 years old. No one can be sure the exact age of an abalone when they grow. Abalone are in much demand by gourmets so they are often priced as high as forty dollars per pound. John's world class specimen yielded more than five pounds, but due to its size, it won't be breaded and sauteed in butter. He donated it to science. Of course, not surprisingly, he treasures the shell. My largest abalone was 9 3/4 inches long, and it was plucked off the rock in only five feet of water at Anchor Bay.

Remember all the large abalone were taken from the ocean north of Fort Bragg. More and more abalone that come out small may be caused by some factors: decreased competition for food and space due to urchin harvesting (remember abalone and urchin don't work together well), increased awareness of the values of abalone stocks and work with Department of Fish and Games who record data collection. The largest abalone can be found in deeper water like 20-40 feet deep or just as easily in rockpicking areas only five feet deep. So only the LUCK can get you the huge abalone! GOOD LUCK!!!

Here are the Top 14 Largest Abalone that were recorded and published by the Department of Fish and Game. The last one was reported on July 1998, and many thanks to Mike Henderson who is an owner of the Anchor Bay Campground.

On the next page is a list of the largest recorded abalone.

Top Largest Abalone

		inches	*metric*	*dates*
1.	John Pepper	12.3	313.4	9/93
2.	Bill Bagasarran	11.9	303.4	8/94
3.	Don Thorpe	11.7	298.6	4/84
4.	Jeff Centoni	11.6	295.0	8/94
5.	Otto Humphrey	11.5	293.0	4/84
6.	Jeff Centoni	11.4	289.0	11/93
7.	Doyle Womack	11.3	287.8	4/91
8.	Jeff Centoni	11.3	287.0	8/94
9.	Dan Mowery	11.2	285.2	10/91
10.	Ralph French	11.1	283.8	6/87
11.	Brad Edwards	11.1	283.0	6/87
12.	Martin Hoben	11.0	281.2	8/94
13.	D.J. Miclette	10.9	278.5	11/90
14.	Felix Macias Jr.	09.7	251.0	5/92

BEST FISH AND
ABALONE STORY
of the Whole Northern California Coast

I have lived here for almost 11 years and have heard hundreds and hundreds of fish stories. I guess, naturally, the tellers are are trying to impress their girlfriends and their wives since the ladies allow them to go fishing or diving. They hope the men can bring fish for their dinners. I am sure you heard of those stories, too. Remember that if you are a fishermen or a diver, you have to tell little lies sometime. But a picture of your catch may prove that you are the best fish story teller...!!!!!

BUCKALONE

Arch Richardson with his prized buckalone. He has plenty of fish stories to show and tell at his business, the Stewarts Point Store.

"BUCKALONE", *Haliotis hornius*, found along the Northern Sonoma Coast (only) between Fort Ross and The Sea Ranch Golf Course in 30 feet of water, not 29' and not 31', then move to that depth as the tides changes. Common but not taken by most divers for two reasons: 1) Most divers do not make it to 30 feet deep. 2) When in the water the horns are soft and pliable and resemble ribbon kelp swaying with the underwater currents and rips. Once pried off the rock, a diver must surface in less than five seconds holding the BUCKALONE in the air for 3 and half minutes to let the horns airdry and set. Some "BUCKALONE" are not noticed as the horns will fall off if not properly air dried.

Taken by Arch Richardson of Stewarts Point, 31ˢᵗ April 1984

WHERE TO FIND ABALONE ON THE NORTH COAST

"**Where is good place to dive for the abalone?**" is what people ask me all the time when I am at work. I have dived all over the North Coast and most places are familiar. Only the best divers know where the big ones are.

I have tried to give you a good list with *mile markers* and *names of locations* on the Sonoma Coast and the Mendocino Coast. There are some things I need to let you know. Please respect all private property! Climb down the cliffs very carefully as they can change during rough weather and crumble at any time. Please do not stand on the edge of the cliff. Take your own trash. There are some good parks and campgrounds where you can change clothes, shower and meet other divers. Please leave everything the same way you came in.

I will start from the south.

• *mile marker* 30.64 — **Red Barn:** It is really a white barn now. However it will always be known as the Red Barn to most. There is a long walk to and a long walk down the cliff, but Red Barn has good abalone along Fort Ross Reef. If you catch four big abalone, be aware that they will be a heavy haul up the cliff. Red Barn has an unpaved parking lot and stairs to climb over the barbed wire that keep the cattle in.

• *mile marker* 31.37 — **Reef Campground:** Operated by State Parks, there are two accesses, both which require paying first. The first one is on the reef bluff. Park in the unpaved parking area, but be aware that it is slippery right after a rain and only has outhouses. It requires a long walk to and down the cliff, to Fort Ross Reef. The other access is to drive down to the campground. There are 20 campsites and bathrooms, first come, first serve. At the end of the campground, park and go to the beach over the hill. There are various places you can dive for abalone with only a short walk. You can bring kayaks here.

• *mile marker* 33.00 — **Fort Ross State Historic Park**, (707) 847-3286. At this site, the Russians built a fort in 1812. State parks added a Visitor Center and museum. Pay first, then keep on driving on past the Visitor Center onto the dirt road. Behind the wood bench is Fort Ross Cove, where you go down the cliff. It is a nice place to dive for abalone, but too popular for most divers. The second access is to drive past the fort to Sandy Cove, where you can unload a boat or kayak and dive. There is a third spot at Fort Ross. Drive past the Visitor Center onto the dirt road and turn right onto the old highway. Go through the gate but be sure to close it to keep the cows inside. Park right after the gate. It is a long walk to the cliff, but there are good abalone from the beach.

• *mile marker* 33.52 — **Old Highway One:** Park on the southbound side of the highway where there is a ladderstair over the fence. There is a 1/4 mile hike to the cliff, then a long hike down, but it is a good abalone dive.

• *mile marker* 33.69 — same as above.

• *mile marker* 34.00 — same as above.

• *mile marker* 34.61 — **Windermere Point:** Park in the unpaved parking area. From there it is a short climb down the cliff. Nearby is Fort Ross Lodge, (707) 847-3333 and a store, (707) 847-3414.

• *mile marker* 35.34 — **Timber Cove Landing and Campground,** (707) 847-3278. There is a good cove down there with nice sized abalone. You can launch a boat there for a fee.

• *mile marker* 37.17 — **Stillwater Cove:** There is a nice cove and a bathroom and changing room are available. Nearby is Stillwater

Cove Regional Campground.

• *mile marker* 37.52 — **North Stillwater Cove:** Park along the road shoulder parking area on the southbound side of the highway. It is a little hike to and down the cliff.

• *mile marker* 38.12 — **Ocean Cove Store and Campground,** (707) 847-3422: One of the best abalone dive camps. There is a boat ramp, too. Down there is a Walsh Cove, where you can either go right or left of the cove for good-sized abalone.

Salt Point State Park (707-847-3221)

• *mile marker* 39.89 — **Gerstle Cove Campground:** There is a campground, day use area, a visitor center and Gerstle Cove Marine Reserve. The road leads to the day use parking lot where there is a changing room and a fish cleaning station. Behind it, is Gerstle Cove Marine Reserve, one of the first underwater parks in California. Abalone diving/fishing is permitted all over the area except in the reserve. A road leads to South Gerstle Cove where you can dive for the abalone, too.

• *mile marker* 40.57 — **North Trail:** Park in the parking lot on the northbound side of the highway. It is a long walk to and short climb down the cliff.

• *mile marker* 41.22 — **Stump Beach:** Park in the parking lot where there is a picnic area with tables and BBQ pits. Stump Beach is the only sandy beach in Salt Point State Park. You have to swim to either the north or south end of the beach to get abalone or go up the hill to the cliff from the beach.

• *mile marker* 42.11 — **South Fisk Mill Cove:** Park in the small road shoulder parking area on the northbound side of the highway. It is a short walk to and short climb down the cliff to the shore.

• *mile marker* 42.36 — **South Fisk Mill Cove:** Same as above, but little shorter and parking is on the southbound side of the highway.

• *mile marker* 42.63 — **Fisk Mill Cove:** Park in the paved parking lot. There are two bathrooms at the end of the road and plenty of picnic areas with BBQs. It is self-pay at the entrance. Go either to South Fisk Mill Cove where there is a path to the beach or to North Fisk Mill Cove and hike down the stairs to the beach, about 1/4 mile.

• *mile marker* 43.06 — **North Fisk Mill:** Park on the southbound side of the road. The hike to and climb down the cliff to the beach is a little long.

• *mile marker* 43.20 — **Old Kruse Barn:** Park along the southbound side of the highway. It is a long hike to the shore.

• *mile marker* 43.66 — **Deadman Gulch:** Park on the southbound side of the highway. Make sure you don't block the gate. It is a long walk to and climb down the cliff to the shore.

• *mile marker* 44.00 — **Horseshoe Point:** Park on the southbound side of the highway. It is a long hike to and climb down the cliff to the shore.

The Richardson property does not allow any trespassers so please obey the law. The Sea Ranch is also private property, although there are four Sonoma County Park beach accesses where you can pay and park to go diving.

Mendocino County

• *mile marker* 4.00 — **South of Anchor Bay:** Park on the southbound side of the highway. It is a very steep climb down the cliff to the shore.

• *mile marker* 4.64 — **Anchor Bay Campground,** (707) 884-4222: It is a private campground (and another good dive camp) with access to the beach, restrooms with a pay shower, fish cleaning station, and a day use parking area. The small town of Anchor Bay is above the campground. The owners are members on the Marine Mammal Center's rescue operations. Abalone diving can be done at either the north or south end of the beach.

• *mile marker* 11.41 — **Schooner Gulch:** Park on the southbound side of the highway. There is a small state park unit and a pit toilet on the trail to the beach.

• *mile marker* 12.35 — **Whiskey Shoals:** Park on the north-bound side of the highway. There is a gate on the private property and a trail to the shore.

• *mile marker* 13.00 — **Moat Creek Surf Access:** There is a parking lot with a trail to the shore. Notice the rock layers along the shore.

• *mile marker* 15.24 — **Point Arena Cove and Pier,** (707) 882-2583: Turn west off the highway onto Port Road to the pier. There is a large parking lot with big pier, small shopping center which includes a restaurant, pizza parlor, and gift shops. Dive on the south side of the beach. The town of Point Arena is nearby.

• *mile marker* 17.00 — **Point Arena Lighthouse and Rollerville Junction Campground,** (707) 882-2440: At the campground turn west towards the lighthouse. The land is privately owned so get the permission to enter. There is lots of rough water along the shore.

• *mile marker* 34.00 — **Greenwood Creek State Beach,** (707) 877-3458: Park in the gravel parking lot on west side of the highway. There is a pit toilet, an old trail down to the shore, a nearby store, gas station and a visitor center nearby.

• *mile marker* 43.93 — **Albion River Campground,** (707) 937-0606: There is a private campground just right off the bridge, a boat ramp, a small store and showers. Dive right off the beach along the cove.

• *mile marker* 48.03 — **Van Damme State Park,** (707)937-0851: There is a state park campground and beach, a parking lot on the west side of the highway, and good abalone diving area despite heavy use by the public. There are pit toilets, outside showers and kayak rental available.

• *mile marker* 49.00 — **Chapman Point:** Park in the small parking area by the fence. It is a small state park property with a very long hike to the shore.

• *mile marker* 49.50 — **Brewery Gulch:** Park in the paved parking area. There is a very steep trail to the beach that makes carrying gear nearly impossible. However, it is a very good dive area.

• *mile marker* 51.00 — **Mendocino Headlands State Park:** Turn west on Little Lake or Main Street to the headland. Park in the parking lot. There is a good access to the shore and beach. Or take Hessel Drive to the loop and parking lot. There is also parking right off the bridge on Lansing Street and Highway 1 and a trail from there down to the shore.

• *mile marker* 52.00 — **Jack Peters Gulch:** Turn west on 500D and park along the road by the fence. Take the trail down the cliff to the beach. Or drive to the end of the road, park and take the trail to the beach.

• *mile marker* 53.00 — **Russian Gulch State Park and Campground,** (707) 937-5804: There is a state park campground and beach, parking lot with restroom and shower and a picnic area nearby. There is good abalone diving up along the shore.

• *mile marker* 54.60 — **South Caspar Point:** On Point Cabrillo Drive, turn west on the hill before or after Caspar Campground. Park in the small lot by the gate. There is a handicapped access to the bluff and a climb down the cliff to dive. This is a residential area so please respect their private property.

• *mile marker* 54.60 — **Caspar Beach,** (707) 964-3306: On Point Cabrillo Drive, there is a large beach with access for kayaks or boat launch. There is a campground nearby that can also handle RVs. The parking area is small but heavily used.

• **Sub-Surface Progression,** (707) 964-3793: It is a full service dive shop on the highway to Fort Bragg.

• **South Harbor Drive Launch Ramp:** There is a boat ramp for boats that can be used for a fee.

• **Noyo Bay and Jetty/Noyo Harbor:** Drive all the way to the end, past the bridge. There is a parking lot, restrooms, and showers for divers. Be careful on the jetty. I prefer to go up on the shore.

• *mile marker* 62.02 — **Glass Beach:** Turn west on Elm Street and go a 1/4 mile to the low bluff. Until the 1960s, the beach was the town dump and is now filled with millions of different colored rounded glass and porcelain pieces.

• *mile marker* 64.90 — **Laguna Point in MacKerricher State Park,** (707) 964-9112: Turn west onto the main road to MacKerricher State Park, continue to the beach parking lot. The abalone diving is not recommended as the area has been overused. However there is nice tidepooling.

• *mile marker* 71.95 — **Kibesillah:** There is a small parking area, and a very, very steep hike down to the beach. Please be very, very cautious! The beach may be washed out during El Niño weather, but check again.

• *mile marker* 79.30 — **DeHaven Creek, Westport-Union Landing State Park,** (707) 964-4406: It is a state park campground open only in summer with a picnic area and pit toilets. At the south part of the park, there is a stair down the bluff to the beach.

• *mile marker* 79.30 — **Abalone Point, Westport-Union Landing State Park:** Go north past the campground to the area where the sign is and park. There is a long stairway to the rocks.

• *mile marker* 83.53 — **Hardy Creek:** The last northern stop I made for abalone diving. There is a small roadside parking area with a good abalone rockpicking place. There are more stops up north that I did not put on my map.

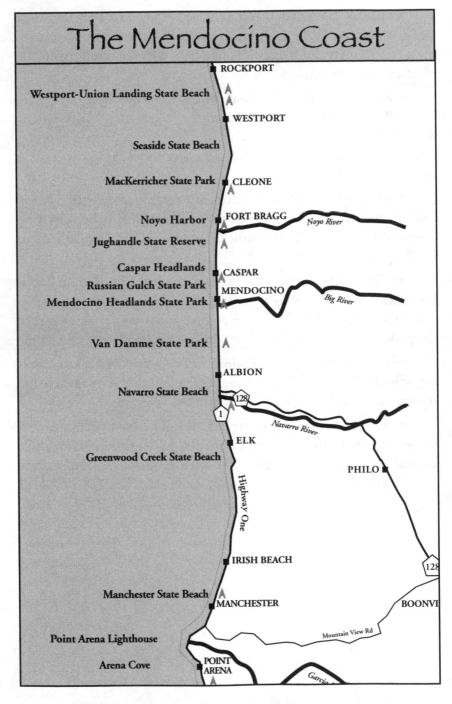

The Mendocino Coast

ROCKPORT

Westport-Union Landing State Beach

WESTPORT

Seaside State Beach

MacKerricher State Park — CLEONE

Noyo Harbor — FORT BRAGG

Noyo River

Jughandle State Reserve

Caspar Headlands — CASPAR

Russian Gulch State Park — MENDOCINO

Mendocino Headlands State Park

Big River

Van Damme State Park

ALBION

Navarro State Beach

128

1

Navarro River

ELK

Greenwood Creek State Beach

PHILO

Highway One

IRISH BEACH

128

Manchester State Beach

MANCHESTER

BOONVI

Mountain View Rd

Point Arena Lighthouse

Arena Cove

POINT ARENA

Garcia

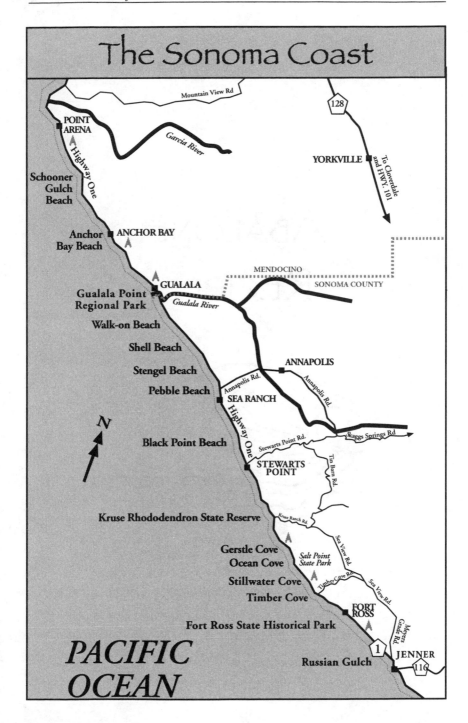

The Sonoma Coast

Mountain View Rd

128

POINT
ARENA

Garcia River

YORKVILLE

To Cloverdale
and HWY. 101

Highway One

Schooner
Gulch
Beach

Anchor ■ ANCHOR BAY
Bay Beach

MENDOCINO

SONOMA COUNTY

GUALALA

Gualala Point
Regional Park

Gualala River

Walk-on Beach

Shell Beach

Stengel Beach

ANNAPOLIS

Pebble Beach

Annapolis Rd.

Annapolis Rd.

SEA RANCH

N

Highway One

Black Point Beach

Stewarts Point Rd.

Skaggs Springs Rd.

STEWARTS
POINT

Tin Barn Rd.

Kruse Rhododendron State Reserve

Kruse Ranch Rd.

Gerstle Cove
Ocean Cove

Salt Point
State Park

Sea View Rd.

Stillwater Cove

Timber Cove Rd.

Sea View Rd.

Timber Cove

FORT
ROSS

Fort Ross State Historical Park

*Meyers
Grade Rd.*

1

JENNER

PACIFIC
OCEAN

Russian Gulch

116

ABALONE
RECIPES

FRIED ABALONE

Famous Deaf Way Abalone Fry
by all Deaf Divers

1 abalone
1 cup of Italian or traditional bread crumbs
2 beaten eggs
olive or cooking oil

Slice the cleaned abalone into 1/4 inch thick steaks. Pound steaks with abalone pounder until the steaks are thinned and easy for quick frying. Try not to pound or tear the meat completely through. Beat eggs well in a bowl and put bread crumbs in another bowl. While the pan is heating up with olive oil or cooking oil, dip the steak in the bowl of beaten eggs, then put in the other bowl of bread. Test if the oil is hot by putting a drop of water in it. If it sputters, then it is ready for frying. Put the abalone in the pan and cook for a minute or so, then turn to other side and cook for another minute or so. Do not overcook as it will be tough and hard to chew. Put cooked steak on a paper towel on the plate to absorb the oil. That is it, and enjoy yourself eating **Deaf Way Cooking Abalone.**

Captain Bob's Italian Abalone

I learned this recipe from an elderly Italian couple in the early 1960s and it has always been a favorite dinner specialty. Keep in mind the extra time involved in the preparation on the abalone steaks is extremely important. After the abalone has been removed from the shell and properly cleaned with 1/8" meat trimmed from bottom of the foot, wrap muscle in "clean" old towel, t-shirt, etc., smack three times each side "top-bottom" with an 18 inch 2"x4". If the meat is splitting, you're hitting too hard. Rinse and slice in 1/4" steaks and then lightly pound on firm surface with flat side of ab iron until it is as tender as a piece of beef.

1 abalone sliced & pounded (covered with milk and stored until ready
to cook)
1-8 ounce package unseasoned french bread crumbs
1/8 cup granulated garlic
1/3 cup chopped parsley
1/4 cup parmesan cheese
1/2 cup vegetable oil

Mix bread crumbs, garlic, parsley, and cheese in large mixing bowl. Heat 1/4" vegetable oil in large frying pan on high heat. Dip abalone in crumb mixture and cook just until brown on each side. Remove and place on a plate covered with paper towels to absorb excess oil. Maintain 1/4" oil in pan and spoon out excess burned bread crumbs — if abalone tends to burn not brown, reduce heat accordingly. Add paper towel over cooked abalone and cover to keep warm. Serve with appropriate side dishes. **Enjoy!**

Silver Seal's Tempura Red Dog Abalone
by Ralph Singleton (Silver Seal)
Padi's first Deaf Scuba Instructor MSDT 67523

Back in the old days of the first Abalone deaf divers, we were at Tomales Bay for camping and beach clamming. Filet (Felix) met us there with some abalone to show us what the hell he was talking about and to lure us much farther north to where he lives. He kinda wanted us to visit his home; but we agreed on a halfway trip to Tomales Bay. We had fun doing clamming, crabbing and fishing. We thought that he was crazy serving up sea snail from his home. But after a long couple of hours of preparing clams, crabs and abalone, we tried the tasty abalone cooked by Felix. After that, we all stormed his territory for regular abalone campouts. We have not set up clamming weekends ever since!

Can you imagine the first period of the Early Deaf Divers Experience? We tried to borrow, rent, or buy equipment to properly accommodate our new diving experience. We bought airplane innertubes as our floats. Of course, it worked but it looked crazy. We had to hike down the treacherous cliffs with all the unnecessary equipment from the city! We found out that we had to bring that stuff back up the high cliffs. We had no choice but to abandon some huge innertubes but never those delicacies, the abalone. We made a pact to come again rain or shine thus we got our namesake "Die Hard Divers". Rough or flat! Filet somehow become our official weatherman over the phone and we learned that rough seas are not a wise day to go out. There is always another day to go!

Camp cooking is usually done with a limited supply of food, ingredients or spices. A well-seasoned, smart diver, would prepare himself by going to the store before the weekend to buy some hot dogs. A back-up Plan B is good to have in case you got skunked or rained out and you still decide to stay the weekend.

A prepared normal diver would bring a bottle of cooking oil, an abalone pounder, frying tongs, eggs and plenty of **BEER**. Time is the thief but worthwhile if you can spend the time cleaning the abalone and find rare pearls in those guts. I have found about 25 pearls so far and have mounted the best of them in gold for my wife as a Christmas surprise! Those empty shells known as **Deaf Ears** are valuable for jewelry, garden decors or used as a California Bathroom soap holder.
2 fully cleaned abalone, sliced and pounded
3 boxes of Dynasty Seafood & Vegetable Tempura Batter
1 bottle of Rosemary Peppercorn Garlic Olive Oil made from Famous Gilroy, California or equal
1 case of Red Dog Beer

Pour 2 cans of Red Dog beer into the tempura batter. Taste the beer (sip) first before pouring for approval. OOPS! Batter looks like a pizza dough, doesn't it? Get that darn 3rd can of Red Dog and remember to grab a sip again! The batter should be as smooth as pancake mix. Heat the cooking oil. Dip the pounded abalone steaks into the batter and drop it into the hot oil. It should look like a pancake. Wait for the surface to dry out and flip it to the other side. Total cooking time is about 7 minutes on each side to get it golden brown. Early Birds to taste those Red Dog Tempura will get to enjoy the rest of the case of beers! You can use any type of soy sauce to add as a dipping sauce.

Caution: Addiction to the Tempura is so great that you will become a Diver. **Good Luck!**

Garbage Abalone
by Mike Burns and his absent-minded friends

Before I say anything about this recipe, we discovered this one at our friend's bachelor party at the Ocean Cove Campground. Due to our idiot, absent-minded friends who did not bring anything to cook our abalone with, we tried to find a way to do it without a stove, nothing to spice it up, and no cookware. Thanks to our brilliant absent-minded friend, he found foil, limes and spices that were supposed to be used to cook the other meat. We cooked the abalone with those limes mixed with other spices, anything else that we could find on the picnic tables, like beer, wine, whiskey (naturally for the bachelor Party), salt, pepper, onions and cheese (supposed to be for our burgers), green pepper, olives, bread crumbs, french dressing, other salad dressing and the spices for our salad, put it in the foil wrapping and cooked it over our campfire. The first word spoken out of our full mouths was "What garbage!" but to tell you the truth, it was the most delicious abalone dinner we ever had, aside from our same old fried abalone dinner. We named the recipe, "Garbage Abalone." Once you do that with anything that would be found on the picnic tables would be your best dinner you will ever have for a long time...**Go ahead and try this recipe!!!!**
1 whole abalone, sliced and pounded (be sure it is tender)
4 limes

1/4 bunch of fresh cilantro
Dash of pepper
1 small whole garlic-chopped
Half chopped yellow onions
1/2 cup red table wine-you added this
Bread crumbs not too much-you added this
1/4 handful of grated parmesan cheese-you added this

Mix all together and let it marniate for minimum 1 hour in ice cold cooler.

Use the wok, lightly spread the pan with olive oil (not extra virgin) cook the abalone not too long, just under 2 minutes. Serve and ready to eat.

You can modify above to make it more interesting. That's why we call this garbage abalone!

If you want you can add the following recipe to the menu.

Crabby Bread

1 French roll
shredded Monterey Jack cheese
shredded meduim cheddar cheese
1 pouchful of imitation crab
Powdered garlic
Dried parsley
Butter

Cut the French roll in half, butter and sprinkle it with powdered garlic. Mix the cheeses, imitation crab and parsley together. Spread them on top of the French roll. Set oven to 375°. Bake the **Crabby Bread** for about 10 minutes or until cheese are nearly melted (do not over melt the cheese). **Enjoy them! Really Yummy!!!**

Abalone-Fresh, Pure and Simple
from Independent Coast Observer, Gualala, CA
By Wendy Platt

1 abalone
1 cup wine or try champagne!
1/3 cup butter
Salt and pepper to taste

Cut abalone into 1/4" slices. Pound with abpounder until the meat is very tender. Place in a bowl and cover with wine. Let sit covered in refrigerator for at least two hours. When ready to serve, melt 1/3 of butter in a frying pan until very hot, but brown. Put in two or three slices of abalone at a time and fry for a minute or so per side. Season as they cook. Add more butter as necessary. Remove from heat and keep warm until all have been cooked. Serve immediately with browned bits that have been accumulated. Serves 4.

Basic Fried Abalone
from a diver at Fort Ross Reef Campground

1 abalone
Flour
Oil

Sprinkle pounded abalone steaks on both sides lightly with flour. Pour 1/4" of cooking oil in large frying pan. Turn burner heat to medium. Let oil get **hot** not just warm. Place abalone steaks into skillet. If steaks start to curl, take a knife and cut a line from the side to the center. The meat will only take a few minutes to cook. Turn regularly until steaks are lightly golden brown. **Overcooking** makes the abalone tough. Place cooked abalone steaks on paper towels to get off excess oil. For a little extra flavor, several strips of bacon can be added to your abalone while cooking.

Famous Filet Abalone Burger

1 abalone
2 cups bread crumbs, preferably Italian style
1 egg
1 cup chopped bell pepper
1 cup chopped onion
1/4 cup butter
sliced cheese (preferably mild)
6 onion roll or burger buns

Cut the whole cleaned abalone into small pieces that can fit into grinder. Grind abalone through meat grinder or electric food grinder. Mix all ground abalone, bread crumbs, egg, bell pepper, and onion. Form into six patties (1/2" thick), then quick-fry in butter until golden brown on both sides. Put slice of cheese over patties. Makes 6 burgers, using mayonnaise, lettuce, tomatoes, ketchup and mustard as preferred. Salt and pepper to taste. Serve 4 to 6 people.

Abalone in Brown Butter
by a camper who always camps at same site
every first weekend of April at Salt Point State Park

1 abalone, sliced and tenderized
2 beaten eggs
2 teaspoons salt/pepper
Butter
Juice of a lemon (or a little more, if desired)
Garlic, squeezed
2 teaspoons capers

Sprinkle abalone slices with salt/pepper. Dip in flour, then dip in eggs. Fry in greased frying pan until both sides are golden brown. Place abalone on serving platter. In a pot, melt butter until browned; remove from heat. Add lemon juice and capers to butter then pour sauce over abalone.

Felix and John Darby, known as Abaloneman, show off our limits in my backyard at Salt Point State Park in 1997

Abaloneman's Red Wine Vinaigarette Abalone
by John Darby
(Winner of 1st Annual Abalone Chef Contest
in 1996 5th Annual ABFEST)

1 good sized abalone, cleaned
1 bottled Marie's Fat Free Red Wine Vinaigarette (vinegar)
1 Contadina Bread crumb (Italian bread crumb)
Olive oil

Slice and pound abalone until tender. Put steaks in a bowl of red wine and marinade and keep it in refrigerate for at least two hours. Coat abalone steak with bread crumbs. Cook steaks in frying pan 30 seconds on each side in olive oil. Place cooked abalone steaks on paper towels to get off excess oil. Serve 4 to 6. **It is one of my favorite recipes and I recommend you try this one. Once you taste it, you can't stop eating!!!!**

Almond Abalone
by Anyomonous

1 abalone, sliced and pounded, large round steak preferred
1/2 cup sliced almonds
1/2 cup (1/4 lb.) butter or margarine, unsalted preferred
All-purpose flour
1/4 teaspoon salt
1/4 teaspoon pepper
1 tablespoon lemon juice

Melt butter over meduim heat in a wide frying pan. Add almonds and cook until butter foams and nuts are lightly browned (5 to 10 minutes). Remove from heat: lift almonds from butter with slotted spoon and set aside. Also set aside with remaining butter.

Gently pat steaks dry with paper towels. Combine flour, salt, and pepper on wax paper or in a shallow pan. Coat steaks with flour mixture: shake off excess. Arrange in single layer on wax paper within reaching distance of range.

Return pan with butter to meduim-high heat: stir in lemon juice and heat until butter begins to foam. Brown abalone steaks, about 30 to 60 seconds on each side, turning once.

When steaks are done, transfer to a warm serving platter. Stir almonds into remaining lemon-butter and pour evenly over steaks. Serve immediately. Makes 4 servings. **I happened to be in the campground while on duty and was asked if I wanted to taste one of their fried steaks. I politely told them that it is against law to feed us or the bears. They insisted that I must eat one of the steaks or they would make big trouble. I accepted immediately, in order to keep them happy. But after I tasted the steak, I started making trouble for them exactly like the bears do when someone tries to eat more of their food. So please do not feed the bears or rangers!!!!!**

Famous Red AbSnapper
by Tom Drabek (Red Snapper)

As Red Snapper always says to me: Abalone can cure your hangover!

On a early morning, I got out of the tent and felt a bit of hangover from the wild, big bonfire party. It was the day of the abalone contest and boy, did I ever look forward to the challenge with my massive hangover. We got the abalone gear in the Zodiac and headed off to a secret spot.

My buddy jumped in the water like a fish, anxious to find some big winner-sized abalone. Here I was still feeling sick as a dog. I finally got in the water and found one legal-sized abalone and popped that baby out and put in the bag. I figured that should do it for the day! I swam back to the boat and just laid in the boat still feeling sick.

Looking at the abalone in the bag, for some reason, the meat looked real refreshing. I took the abalone out of the bag and placed it against my head. Boy, did I ever feel good and relieved. Ten minutes later, my hangover had disappeared!

I gave the abalone a real long kiss and the next thing I knew this abalone was trying to tell me something. I looked at her and understood what she was trying to tell me. I jumped into water and got my limit. The next thing I knew I had won the biggest abalone contest!

So if you want to find some big abalone for the contest: first you must give a nice, long, juicy kiss to that slimy meat, give her a hug, then maybe she'll show ya the way to the biggest abalone. This is one of my few secret tricks!!!!

1 whole abalone
1 whole can bread crumbs
3 tablespoons garlic powder:
42 shakes of black pepper
5 tablespoons rosemary
4 eggs
Olive oil

Slice abalone to 3/16" thick and pound. Coat with egg first then in bread crumbs with all spices. Prepare to cook in olive oil for only one minute and 42 seconds per side. Then check it out to eat but first have a cold beer and a fiesta! **This always happens every time we get together camp and dive right here!**

Other Basic Fried Abalone
in different way
by the campers I met and ate with
at Ocean Cove Campground
and Salt Point State Park

1 clean abalone, cut into 1/4" thick
Either flour or bread crumb
2 cups of oil: olive, vegetable, or canola oil
or
Butter or Margarine or I Can't Believe It's Butter-(Unsalted butter
   tends not to burn as quickly)

Clean, slice and tenderize abalone. Heat in a large frying pan with either oil or butter. Make sure it is real **HOT**. Cover abalone steak with flour or bread crumbs. Fry in frying pan until golden brown on both sides. Do not overcook! Put abalone on papertowel to remove excess oil. Serves 2-4.

Some options:

(1) For better taste, add three or four strips of bacon during cooking **OR**

(2) Marinate abalone in 1 cup wine for one hour or little longer right after cutting and pounding **OR**

(3) Add 1/4 sesame seeds and 1/8 teaspoon cayenne **OR**

(4) After covering abalone steak with flour or bread crumbs, prepare a mix of 2 well beaten eggs, 1/4 cup of milk, 1/2 can beer, 1 teaspoon salt, 1 teaspoon baking powder. Whip until thickened. Dip steaks in this mixture, then fry in oil.

Abalone and Gravy
by Vivian Wilder and Violet Chappell
Our Mother's Recipe,
Essie Parrish, Spiritual Leader of Kashia

For 2 abalone
Slice and tenderize
1/2 green onions, chopped, (optional)
1/2 cup flour
1 teaspoon salt
1 teaspoon black pepper
1 to 2 cups of water

Combine 1/2 cup flour and salt/pepper in bowl. Cover both sides of abalone with flour. Brown abalone on both sides. Repeat until all abalone is cooked. Transfer abalone on to a platter.

Add 1 to 2 cups of water to abalone drippings and stir. Add abalone back to pan. Stir abalone to make gravy. Then add green onions, (optional).

Abalone Ritz
by Gloria Frost of Ocean Cove

1 abalone
1 cup crushed Ritz crackers
1/4 cup Italian seasoned bread crumbs
1 egg
2 teaspoons water
Hot oil

Clean, slice, and pound slices with a mallet. In a pie pan, place 1 cup finely crushed Ritz crackers, (place crackers in ziplock bag, roll with rolling pin). Add 1/4 cup Italian seasoned crumbs to crushed crackers.

In a shallow bowl, mix 1 egg and 1 teaspoon water, beat thoroughly. Dip ab slice in egg, let excess drip off then place in cracker/

crumb mix. Coat each side. Place on cookie sheet covered with wax paper. When all are coated, carry to the stove. Fry in 3/4 cup hot oil for one minute on each side or just until golden. EAT UP!

Abalone Louise with Cheese Sauce
by Steve Gutierrez of Gualala, California

4 to 6 abalone steaks, sliced and pounded until tender, (big steaks work better)
3 eggs, beaten
1 1/2 cup of seasoned bread crumb
1/3 cup of olive oil
1 cup of small shrimp, peeled and cooked
1 cup crab meat

While heating up the frying pan with olive oil, dip the steaks in bowl of beaten eggs first, then to bowl of bread crumb. Fry the steak until golden brown (usually 30 seconds per side). Remove from the pan, fill with crab and shrimp. Roll up and place in dish cover with cheese sauce and serve hot!!!!

Cheese Sauce

Make your own cheese sauce or use Aunt Mary's white sauce and add American cheese slices. Blend well in sauce pan.

Hawaiian Magic Patties
by Lorenzo Jamito Jaquias

Note: Ahola! As a long time North Coast abalone diver, surfer, and a maintenance worker at Salt Point State Park, I live on all seafood and surf 365 days a year.
1 cleaned abalone

1/2 pound bacon strips
1 egg
1 cup bread crumbs
1/2 cup onion, chopped
Salt and pepper
1 teaspoon oyster-flavored sauce

Clean ab and cut to 1/4" strips to grind through a hand grinder. Grind bacon, too. Mix ab and bacon in a bowl, then add egg, crumbs, onions, oyster sauce (add more if you want), salt and pepper. Mix well until it looks like hamburger. Makes about a dozen patties. Brown both sides in vegetable oil. **Do not overcook.** Serve with steamed rice and vegetables.

Abalone in Cream
by Old woman who grew up in Northern California who comes here to camp once a year

7 pound abalone steak, (she must be a real old woman because a 7
    pounder is a BIG abalone and rarely found around here, or maybe
    it was a huge one in the old days)
egg
salt and pepper
cracker crumbs
1 cube butter (1/2 cup)
1/2 cup cream
7 teaspoons lemon juice

Bread abalone steaks with egg and cracker crumbs, add salt and pepper. Cut into bite-sized pieces. Heat butter in frying pan until golden brown (about 1 minute on each side). When all pieces are fried, add cream and lemon juice. Cook until cream is all heated (about 30 seconds). Place in chafing dish and provide fondue forks or tooth-picks for abalone pieces.

NOTE: Abalone was abundant when I was a kid growing up in Northern California. Now, my children have never tasted abalone just fished from these cold waters. Calamari is a substitute — though it misses the flavor, it does have that same characteristic texture. Take calamari steak and tenderize with a mallet as you would abalone. The mallet can be wood or metal but it should have "prongs".

Easy's Abalone and Asparagus Fettucine
by 'Easy Ed Vodrazka'

Note: Being lifeguards on the North Coast, we end up preparing a lot of abalone for guests who come up to visit from all over the state. For us, preparation time becomes an issue. The thing I love about this recipe is that the ab preparation is so easy. You don't have to be careful when you tenderize the steaks.

Side note: This is an exceptional recipe if you're cooking to impress a date...Believe me, after the first scrumptious bite, your guest will be thoroughly convinced that you can actually cook. From that point on, you're on your own.

For two people, this is enough for an excellent dinner and lunch the following afternoon.

A good Chardonnay
An average sized abalone
1 pound of asparagus (cut into inch long pieces)
1 large onion (chopped)
A handful of sun-dried tomatoes, chopped
1-1/2 pounds fettucine noodles
1 large spoonful curry
2 spoonfuls chicken bouillon in 3/4 cup water
1/4 cup butter
1 cup milk
1/3 cup Wondra flour

Egg mixture:
1 egg beaten with 1 large spoonful of the curry, 1 teaspoon each of
salt and pepper, dab of milk

Cut abalone into 1/4" thick steaks and pound recklessly (it doesn't
matter if the meat tears). Cut the pounded steaks up into bite-sized
pieces (again they don't have to be pretty). Soak the ab in the egg
mixture for an hour or so. Open the Chardonnay, put your favorite
Bill Evans CD on the player and pour a glass for yourself and your
company.

Then later…Heat a little canola oil and add onions, bouillon
and remaining curry (start water heating for the fettucine). When the
onions are clear, add the abalone pieces. Cook the abalone, stirring
often until it's cooked through (around 12 minutes). Add asparagus
and sun-dried tomatoes and mix them in with the hot abalone for a
minute or two. Turn the heat down to simmer and watch the asparagus, when the asparagus is cooked but still firm, stir in the milk. Finally, thicken with the Wondra flour by sprinkling it in slowly. Put
the finished abalone mixture aside and keep it warm while you cook
the fettucine (this allows the flavors of abalone mixtures to settle in
together).

Take the fettucine off while it's still 'al dente,' don't rinse it. Ladle
the abalone asparagus mixture over a bed of fettucine noodles. By this
time you might have to open that second bottle of Chardonnay that
you keep in the back of the fridge for emergencies. Find your second
favorite Bill Evans CD, put it on, and sit down to a wonderful meal.

Felix, Ramiro Garcia and Mike Sutherland with lobster caught at the Channel Islands in 1998. Lobster can be prepared using the recipe, Abalone with Seafood Roll.

Abalone with Seafood Roll
for the person who has the hot date and have to impress his date with his cooking

4 or 5 large abalone steaks, sliced and tenderized
2-3 loster tail, cleaned out and sliced
1 crab, not in season, then try for a can of crabmeat
1/2 lb. of shrimp
1 clove garlic
butter
white sauce, a recipe to follow

Melt the butter in a medium sauce pan, cook the lobster tail, crab meat and shrimp for a quick few minutes (2-3 minutes), but do not overcook. Remove them and set aside. Cook abalone steaks in sauce pan for few seconds (45 seconds to 1 minute, but do not cook over 1 minute). Brush steaks with white sauce, then dip a scoop of shellfish mix in white sauce and put on top of each steak. Roll steak and put toothpick to hold steak together. Brush with remaining white sauce. Put rolled steaks on broiler and brown lightly. **Serve with your best wine and French bread. Include a vase of flower and candle on a table. Dim the lights. Your date will be more impressed or flattered with your cooking and sea life romance!!**

White Sauce:
3 tablespoons melted butter
3 tablespoons sifted flour
1/4 teaspoon salt
1/4 teaspoon pepper
1 cup milk

In a pot, combine butter with flour, thoroughly. Add milk, stirring vigorously. Bring mixture to a boil. Reduce heat. Add salt and pepper. Cook 1 minute longer, stirring constantly. Makes a cup.

Abalone Stuffed With Crabmeat
by Anonymous but too delicious to be ignored

White Sauce
2 tablespoons butter or margarine
2 tablespoons flour
salt and pepper
1 cup warm milk

Abalone
butter or margarine
2 shallots, minced
1 cup crabmeat
salt and pepper

1 dash red pepper
1/2 teaspoon dry mustard
1/2 teaspoon Worcestershire sauce
1/2 lemon (juice only)
4 large abalone steaks
2 eggs, beaten
flour

Melt butter in skillet and stir in flour. Season to taste with salt and pepper. Cook, stirring, over meduim heat about 1 minute but do not allow flour to brown. Add milk and cook and stir 1 or 2 minutes until mixtures comes to boil and thickens. Set aside.

For abalone, melt butter in small saucepan, add shallots and cook until tender but not browned. Add crabmeat and heat thoroughly. Add enough white sauce to bind, about 1/2 cup. Season to taste with salt and pepper and add red pepper, mustard, worcestershire and lemon juice. Carefully pound abalone steaks between 2 sheets of waxed paper until very thin. Dip abalone in eggs seasoned to taste with salt and pepper. Coat with flour and set aside. Melt butter in heavy skillet. Add abalone and brown quickly on one side. Turn and brown other side. Do not overcook as abalone will toughen. Place abalone steaks on platter and spoon crabmeat stuffing on each. Roll and arrange on serving platter; seam down. If desired, serve with any remaining sauce. **Too good to be ignored, and will be gone real quick when served.**

BAKED ABALONE

Baked Abalone a la Martin
by The Abalone Book

1 whole abalone, cleaned, not sliced
1/2 cup cooking oil
1/2 cup flour
1 teaspoon salt
1 teaspoon pepper
1/2 dry white wine
1/2 cup water
1 freshly minced garlic clove
1 teaspoon cornstarch

Pound all surfaces of abalone carefully, retaining its upside-down mushroom shape. Smear with oil, then sprinkle on flour, salt and pepper. Brown lightly in frying pan, then place in casserole dish. Add wine, water and minced garlic, then cover and bake for 30-40 minutes at 375°. Slice into 3 or 4 pieces before serving. Juice may be thickened with cornstarch if gravy is desired. Feeds 2 to 4 persons.

You Can Bake Abalone in Wine
by Timothy P. given to me at Albion Campground at Albion

1 abalone
1 cup white wine or little more if you want
2 stalks celery, finely chopped
1/4 teaspoon cream of tartar
Salt and pepper
4 tablespoons butter
2-6 ounce cans of white sauce

Mix the above ingredients in a small mixing dish. Wrap in a towel and pound whole abalone all over very well. Place the ab in a baking dish. Cover with the mixture. Cover the baking dish and bake for one hour at 350°. Let abalone stand for one or two hour before eating. **This is really very good tasting. I had this with campers that camped next to me.**

Filet's Baked Abalone

1 whole cleaned abalone
1 can cream of mushrooms
1/2 can water
1/2 cup chopped onion, can add more if you like to taste more onion
1/2 cup chopped celery
dash of pepper
Flour
3 large potatoes, peeled and cut in half

Clean and carefully pound whole abalone with big mallet or use abpounder with smooth side only, until it is tender. Sprinkle flour over entire abalone. Fry whole abalone until lightly browned. Wipe off excess oil. Mix cream of mushroom, water, onion, celery, and pepper and place abalone in a glass baking pan and cover with the mixture. Add potatoes at after first 15 minutes and bake again for 45 minutes (one hour baking total). Serves 3-4 persons.

Abalone Jerky
by State Park Lifeguard

1 whole abalone, trimmed
4 beef or chicken bouillon cubes
2 teaspoons ground pepper
8 teaspoons salt
2 quarts salt water

Put abalone in a pot filled with salt water. Add 4 bouillon cubes and pepper, then boil for one hour. Cut meat into thin strips. To dry, put in oven rack at lowest heat overnight or until strips are dry, or else wrap in cheesecloth and dry for at least one week in hot sun. Make about 12 strips of jerky. **He gave them to me on his lunch and I liked them, go and try it!!!**

Abalone Pizza
by Ed Whitt
author of Cooking Abalone and
owner of Rohnert Park Dive Center (707) 584-2323

1 abalone
1 cup flour
4 teaspoons butter
2 beaten eggs
Topping as desired: marinara sauce, olives, onions, oregano, parsley and mozzarella cheese

Prepare abalone as you would for frying. Fry only long enough to hold batter to the meat. Use abalone as you would pizza dough. Add your favorite toppings. Bake in pre-heated oven at 350° for 10-15 minutes or cheese has melted. **I have tried this and like it very much! It is one of my recommended list for all of you to try! You can grind the abalone through meat grinder instead of pounding and cutting into small pieces.**

Baked Abalone
by Lazy Divers like me

1 clean whole abalone
2-3 slices bacon
Juice from 1/2 lemon

Clean and tenderize abalone. Lay bacon over abalone, squeeze few drops of lemon juice over it and wrap in aluminum foil. Bake at

350° for about 40 minutes. Unwrap abalone and baste with juice left over in the foil. Bake uncovered for another 10 minutes. When done, slice abalone and serve with lemon or tartar sauce. Serves 4. It was one of my fastest, easiest recipes as it doesn't require any dishes to wash. I recommend you try this LAZY recipe!!

Lemon Hab
by Dave Verno
owner of Timber Cove Boat Landing (707) 847-3278

1 or 2 whole abalone, pounded and scored on both sides
1 can cream of mushroom soup
1 cup fresh sliced or can of mushrooms
1 tablespoon minced garlic
2 slices lemon
chopped onions

Rub scored abalone with butter and minced garlic. Place in aluminum foil. Add all above ingredients. Close foil tightly. Bake at 350° for one hour.

Abalone A La Fathom
by Gloria Frost of Ocean Cove

1 abalone
Lemon Juice
Garlic
Onion

Remove ab from the shell. Remove guts. Wash then serrate in tic-tac-toe pattern. Wrap in burlap bag. Slam 6-8 times on, each side with 2x4. Wash.

Soak abalone in lemon juice for 1/2 to 1 hour. Stuff serrated slits with garlic, onion, bay leaf, etc. Put ab in a Dutch oven in the oven.

Bake for 45 minutes to 1 hour at 350.° Aluminum foil also works. Your abalone should be the consistency of cheesecake.

BBQ ABALONE

Filet's BBQ Abalone by Filet

1 clean abalone
3-4 strips bacon
Onion, chopped
Any sauce like Teriyaki sauce, Soy Sauce
or
Wine, 1/2 cup
Salt and pepper
All spices you like to add to taste

Build a large wood fire in fire-ring or on beach in rock-lined pit or in BBQ. Clean, and pound a whole abalone with 2x4 board or abalone pounder (smooth one) until it is soft. Score the abalone several times with 1/2" deep slits on both sides. Place bacon strips in first, then seasoning, onions, sauce or wine. Put abalone on top, then a top layer of onion, sauce or wine, then last bacon. Wrap abalone with foil and place foil-wrapped abalone on grill. Make sure it doesn't too get close to the fire as it will burn inside the foil. Turn the abalone over often. It will take 45 minutes to cook. Open the foil to check. Take juices from inside the foil and spread over abalone. Cover foil and put back on grill and cook for 10-15 more minutes. Slice into bite-sized pieces. Serves 2-4. **It is another one of my easy ways to cook without washing any dishes. Perfect for campers who just got in from diving.**

Oriental Grilled Abalone
by Rex Barlow
(Winner of 2nd Annual Abalone Chef Contest
in 1997 6th Annual ABFEST)

2 pounds of fresh abalone or swordfish
2 scallions, minced
1 tablespoon grated fresh ginger
1 tablespoon soy sauce

1 tablespoon sake or dry sherry
1 tablespoon peanut oil or cooking oil
1/2 teaspoon raw brown sugar
1/2 teaspoon salt

Thaw abalone or swordfish, if frozen, using sharp knife to cut to small pieces.

For seasoning mixture, combine scallions, ginger, soy sauce, sake, oil, sugar, salt. Rub meat with some of mixture. Rub remaining seasonings into the slits. Let stand at room temperature more than an hour. Shake seasoning off the meats and place into a plastic bowl with a good cover for every 15 minutes. Charcoal: Indirect Gas: Indirect/ Medium Heat

Lightly grease cooking grill. Place meats in center of the cooking grill. Grill about a few minutes until the meat becomes tender, when tested with fork. **NOTE:** Scoring helps the meats absorb the blend of seasoning during grilling. **Very delicious! No wonder he won the contest!!!!!!!!**

Bar-B-Q Ab
by Timber Cove Boat Landing (707) 847-3278

1/4 pound butter
1/2 cup lemon juice
pinch pepper and paprika
abalone steaks, pounded

Melt the butter and add the lemon juice, pepper, and paprika. Stir. Dip each ab steak into this mixture and then place it on the barbecue grill. Turn frequently, basting with the mixture before each turn, cooking until the steak just begins to stiffen.

Six of these per person should be plenty. And for you cowards who really can't handle the out-of-doors, these can also be done in a preheated 400° oven for 2 minutes in a lightweight pan.

BBQ-Abalone on the Shell
by a real cool camper at Salt Point State Park

1 clean abalone, wrap in towel and hit with flat mallet, do it again
after turn it over, do it about 3-4 times
1 very clean **shell**
1/4 cup dry wine
garlic, minced or squeezed
Any seasoning like salt, pepper, any spices
Aluminum foil

Slit 1/2" deep slices all over the abalone, both sides of the abalone, much as you can. Place cleaned shell on large aluminum foil
and put abalone with all ingredients on shell. Seal the foil around
abalone and place on grill. Barbecue for 40-50 minutes depending on
how hot the fire is.

The taste of shell adds a nice flavor to this recipe.

Before you make this recipe, make sure you clean the shell very
well, being sure to scrub on the top of the shell. If not, the kelp or dirt
will come with your dinner!

BBQ Abalone on Grill
from an Old Timer who lived here on the coast too long

1 whole abalone
4 teaspoons flour
1/2 teaspoons salt
1/2 teaspoons pepper
1 clove garlic, minced or chopped
1/2 cup cream
1 strip bacon

Pound a whole abalone until tender, work in flour, salt, and pepper. Place in heavy foil, add garlic, bacon, and cream and seal foil
well, being sure to seal out the air, also. Place on a barbecue grill,

medium heat, cook for 45 minutes. Can be cooked in casserole (without foil). Serves 2-4. **This recipe convinced Tom Drabek to come up here many times and bang on my door after his first taste of this abalone recipe. Try it and you will come and bang on my door, too!**

Sweet BBQ (Burns BBQ) Abs
by Michael Burns (Aquaman)
(Placed Second at 1st Annual Abalone Chef Contest in 1996 5th Annual ABFEST)

2 garlic cloves
3 tablespoons low sodium soy sauce
2 teaspoons honey
2 teaspoons maple syrup
3 teaspoons sesame oil
2 tablespoons Cilantro
1 abalone

About 4 quart bowl, combine garlic, soy sauce, honey, maple, sesame oil and cilantro, and mix well. Set it in refrigerator or place in the cold ice chest while preparing abalone.

Clean the abalone (see Filet's abalone cleaning instructions). Cut thin slices and clean them with fresh running water. Pat dry the abalone and place them in the mixed sauce. Marinate the abalone for 30 minutes or more or overnight.

Remove the abalone from the sauce and place in a large saucepan. Cook until done. Do not overcook otherwise you will be eating rubberbands!

Place the cooked **SWEET BBQ ABS** over the cooked rice. Enjoy my **SWEET BBQ ABS**!

Stuffed Bull Kelp Abalone
by Ranger Jerry Loomis of Point Lobos State Reserve

Before I wrote this recipe, I ran into a ranger who raved about a great dinner he had with another ranger who happened to be picking abalone around here at Fort Ross. He told me that I had to get the recipe from the ranger who used bull kelp to cook the abalone over a campfire. Seemed like it would be very simple to cook, and sure enough it was most delicious I had ever eated without the benefit of cookware to cook the abalone with. All you do is dive for some good ol' abalone and cut several strips of bull kelp about two feet long. Don't waste that bull kelp too much as all ocean living things depend on the bull kelp to survive. Just cut what you would need. Here's the recipe you should like to try.

<u>Stuffed Bull Kelp Abalone:</u> Cut a few bull kelp tubes about two feet long. Pound the abalone into appoximately 1 square inch pieces. Stuff the kelp tubes with abalone and a mix of white wine, garlic (squeezed or cut into small pieces) and lemon juice until it is full. Plug the end of tube with piece of dowel or broom handle to seal the hole. Cook on a open fire, grill or coals until the kelp tube is charred. Serve by slitting the tube lengthwise. **Very good dinner!!!!** **Point Lobos State Reserve is one of the best and most beautiful dive places in Monterey so go check yourself. You will love that place!!! <u>Sorry</u>, no abalone or marine animals may be taken out of the reserve.**

SOUPS & CHOWDERS

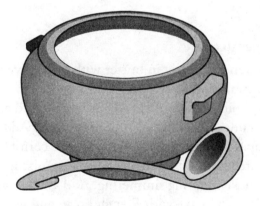

Filet's Famous Abalone Chowder

1 cleaned abalone (preferred 1/2 abalone through meat grinder and
    other 1/2 sliced, pounded and cut in small pieces)
3 to 4 potatoes, cut into 1" cubes
1 large onion, chopped
2-3 stalks celery, thinly sliced
1/2 cup olive oil
1/4 teaspoon dill weed
1/2 teaspoon sweet basil
1/2 quart (16 ounces) low fat or regular milk
1 can evaporated milk
8 or more ounces water, enough to cover potatoes
2-3 bouillon cubes (preferably vegetable)
1/2 cup extra milk
Cornstarch
1 can of clams
Salt and pepper to taste

    Cook onion and celery in butter with little olive oil. When it is
ready, add spices, clam juice from can, potatoes, and onion/celery
mix. Bring to boil and simmer for 15 minutes. Add abalone, clams,
and bouillon cubes, cook for 5-10 more minutes. Add 12-16 ounces
milk and evaporated milk. **Do not boil,** mix cornstarch with extra
milk in separated bowl until dissolved. Add to mixture when close to
a boil, soup thickens during simmering. Add salt and pepper to taste.
Makes 6 to 8 bowls. Serve with French bread and wine.

Suzanne Westover, Salt Point Ranger, and our great salmon guide and camphost, Jim Vlavianos, bragged with three salmon, about 18 pounds each, caught 200 yards off Salt Point.

Filet's World Famous Abalone and All-Star Seafood Cioppino

1 cleaned abalone (preferred 1/2 abalone for grinding and other for sliced, pounded, cut to small pieces)
1 large onion, cut into small slices
2 cloves garlic, pressed
3/4 cup chopped parsley
3 cups bell peppers, each cup in red, yellow and green bell peppers

1 can (15 ounces) tomato sauce
1 can (28 ounces) tomatoes (preferably Italian style)
1 cup red wine, inexpensive wine preferred as it dissolves well
1 bay leaf
1 teaspoon dry basil
1/2 teaspoon dry oregano leaves
1 can clams
1 can crab, if Dungeness crab, get two of them and cleaned and cracked
Shrimp
Any catch of the day **fish**, would be nice, too

In a large stock pot, mix oil, onion, garlic, bell peppers, and parsley; cook over medium heat, stirring often until onion and bell peppers are soft. Stir in tomato sauce, tomatoes, wine, bay leaf, basil, and oregano. Cover and simmer until a little thickened, about 15-20 minutes. Add clams, crab, shrimp, and abalone and simmer for 10 minutes or more. Makes 6 to 8 bowls. Serve with French bread and wine. **Very good soup!!!!!**

Cioppino
by Don Hoard, Salt Point State Park Visitor Center Volunteer

1 large onion, chopped (about 1 cup)
1 medium-sized green pepper, halved, seeded and chopped
1/2 stalk sliced celery
1 carrot, peeled and grated
3 cloves of garlic, minced
3 tablespoons olive oil
2 cans (1 pound each) tomatoes
1 can (8 ounces) tomato sauce
1 teaspoon leaf basil, crumbled
1 bay leaf
1 teaspoon salt
1/4 teaspoon pepper

1 pound frozen halibut or turbot
1 dozen mussels in shell, if available **OR:** 1 can (10 ounces) clams in
   shell
1-1/2 cups dry white wine
1 package (8 ounces) frozen, shelled, deveined shrimp
1/2 pound fresh or frozen scallops
2 tablespoons minced parsley
1 small abalone, grinded through the meat grinder

    1. Sauté onion in a kettle or dutch oven the green pepper, celery, carrot and garlic in olive oil until soft. **2.** Stir in tomatoes, tomato sauce, basil, bay leaf, salt and pepper; heat to boiling: lower heat; cover; simmer for 2 hours. Discard bay leaf. **3.** While sauce simmers, remove the skin from the halibut or turbot, cut into serving-size pieces. Using a stiff brush, thoroughly scrub the mussels, cutting off their "beards" under running water to remove any residue of mud and sand. Reserve for use in Step 5. **4.** Stir wine into the sauce in the kettle. Add the fish, shrimp and scallops. Simmer, covered, 10 minutes longer. **5.** Place mussels or clams in a layer on top of fish in kettle, cover, steam 5 to 10 minutes, or until the shells are fully opened and fish flakes easily. (Discard any unopened mussels). **6.** Ladle into soup plates or bowls. Sprinkle with parsley. Serve with sourdough bread, or crusty French or Italian bread. Makes 8 servings.

    NOTE: If fresh clams are available and reasonably priced, use 1 dozen in place of the canned clams. Be sure to rinse them well before adding to soup, and discard any that do not open once they have been cooked.

    OPTION: Add 1/2 cooked crab per person during last 5 minutes. Add 1 small **abalone**, preferably ground, during last 5 minutes. **I tried it and the soup was so good and so delicious. Very long work, but very worth it for dinner on a rainy and cold night.**

Abalone Chowder
My Grandmother, Mercedes Call's Recipe
By Barbara Black

George W. Call, born in Ohio, became a businessman after coming to California in 1852. Later he travelled widely, and in 1873 he and his Chilean wife, Mercedes, and their family moved from South America to Fort Ross. They invested in land until they owned 8,000 acres. The Call Family ranched Fort Ross for 100 years and operated Fort Ross Hotel, making it a social center and resort. In 1903, California Historical Landmark League bought 2.45 acres on which the fort itself stood. Three years later, the league deeded the property to the State of California. Subsequent purchases from the Call Family have enlarged Fort Ross State Historic Park to more than 735 acres.

from the Fort Ross Visitor Center

Please visit Fort Ross State Historic Park as it has lots of places to look and learn…

1 good-sized abalone
4 large potatoes
4-5 slices of bacon
1 large onion
1/2 gallon of regular milk
salt to taste
coarse ground pepper

This is one of those recipes you learn from mother to daughter. I first start with the potatoes: boil and mash them. Cut 4 to 5 slices of bacon into pieces and put in a medium-sized pot to fry. Add 1 large onion and sauté with the bacon. When the onion is tender, add 1/2 gallon of milk and salt to taste. Have a good-sized abalone pounded whole and cut into 1/2" squares. When the milk, onion and bacon are hot, add mashed potates. Bring to the desired heat. Add coarse ground pepper. Have a bowl of finely chopped Italian parsely and garnish each bowl of chowder with this. Hope you try this. Ths recipe has been passed from grandmother to mother to daughter for over 125 years.

North Coast Lifeguard's Best Abalone Chowder
from 'Easy' Ed Vodrazka

Note:

The beauty of this hearty chowder is that it requires very little work with the abalone, and it tastes wonderful! Also, it works well with those frozen abalone that never taste as good as fresh ones when you prepare them fried in garlic or breaded in the traditional way. This is a winter favorite in our house!

You can replace the canned corn and peas with fresh, but this is the easy way
A good Chardonnay
1 loaf of good sourdough bread
1 medium sized ab (for us lifeguards, that's anything over 9")
3 large onions
7 or 8 medium potatoes, chopped in small cubes
2 cans of corn
1 can of peas
Wondra sauce and gravy flour
1 quart. milk (your choice...you could go cream if you really want to be decadent)
4 stalks of celery
7 cubes of chicken bullion
1/4 cup butter
Mustard, a spoon or two
Seasonings (I use thyme, pepper, salt, curry)
Canola oil

Pound the ab whole, maybe 10 times a side. No need to be fancy about it...then cut it up and grind it in a meat grinder. Dissolve the bullion cubes in about 3 quarts. of hot water...set aside. In the largest frying pan or wok you have, brown the onions slowly in the butter with a little Canola oil, then add some of the broth (maybe a cup) and the mustard and seasonings of choice. Add all of the abalone, cook on medium to high heat for around 8 minutes. Put aside. Meanwhile, boil potatoes in remaining broth until tender, but not mushy. Reduce heat on potatoes and add the abalone. Simmer around 15 minutes or so. Reduce heat to warm and add celery, peas, corn. Add milk slowly, and finally, sprinkle in the Wondra to thicken it up (remember that the thickening is delayed, so add a little at a time, and stir constantly to avoid clumping). Adjust seasonings and serve with warm sourdough bread. If you've got the patience, this soup will taste even better if you make it a few hours before supper time and just keep it warm. Remember to say your prayers before eating...'cause this is as close to heaven as you can get on this earth!

Abalone Chowder
By Dan Winkelman
(He used to work as a ranger at Salt Point, now at Angel Island)

1 onion, chopped
2 stalks celery, chopped
2 slices bacon
2 tablespoons butter
2 small red potatoes
2 or 3 cups abalone, chunks
1 cup white wine or chicken broth
2 cups milk or Half & Half

Cook onions and celery in butter until soft, but not brown, partially boil potatoes. Drain liquid into a large pot. Add onion and celery, add potatoes and bacon (1/2" strips) and abalone. Simmer 2-3 hours. Add wine when thickening. When abalone is tender, add milk and simmer for 1/2 hour. Do not boil milk.

Yummy Abalone Soup!
by Bernice Singleton
(a deaf mother of First Deaf Scuba Instructor)

12 slices bacon, chopped
1 abalone, minced and fried with breadcrumbs
8 cups peeled and diced potatoes
4 small onions, chopped
1 cup flour
8 cups milk
3 cups light cream (half and half)
4 teaspoons salt or less
1 teaspoon pepper
2 cups celery
2 cups carrots, chopped

Fry bacon. Use grease for frying abalone with breadcrumbs. Then cook all ingredients in a large pot. **Yummmmmy!**

Dan Murley and Bill Walton, with over 40 years of Parks Services between them work as rangers at Fort Ross State Historic Park. They decided to play hooky for the first time after seeing the ocean so calm and flat. They caught cabezeos, lingcods, many rockfish and abalone at the Fort Ross Cove.

MEXICAN ABALONE

Filet's Famous Mexican Rolled Abalone
by Filet

1 whole clean abalone
1 can of whole green chile, mild, but if you like hot , then choose
    spicy hot
Monterey Jack cheese, sliced
1 beaten egg
1 can of Italian bread crumb
Cooking oil or olive oil
Wooden toothpicks

Slice abalone about 3/16 inch thick and pound. Dip steaks in bowl of beaten eggs then in a bowl of bread crumbs. Slice the whole green chiles into two or three pieces, and put on the abalone steak with slice of cheese. Roll and secure with one or two wooden toothpicks. Heat oil in frying pan until it is very hot. Cook for at least one minute or two per side. Place on paper towel to dry off excess oil. **It is one of my favorite recipes and I heartily recommend it to you! It can be baked in uncovered casserole dish for 15 minutes at 350° instead of frying!**

Filet's Other Famous Mexican Rolled Abalone

1 whole clean abalone
1 can of green chiles
Monterey Jack, sliced or 1/2 grated
1 beaten egg
1 can of bread crumbs
Butter
Wooden toothpicks
Salsa, about 12 ounces, I prefer Safeway Select, Garlic Lover's Salsa
    (medium)
1 small onion, finely chopped
1 clove garlic. minced
1 large avocado

Slice abalone about 3/16" thick and pound. Dip steaks in bowl of beaten egg then a bowl of bread crumbs. Slice the whole green chile into two or three pieces and put on the steak with a slice of cheese. Roll and secure with one or two toothpicks. Quick-fry in butter until light golden brown. Put rolled steaks in casserole dish and spread salsa, garlic, and onion on rolled abalone. Cover with grated cheese and avocado. Bake at 350° until cheese is really melted. Serve with Spanish rice for 2 to 4 people. Try **it and you will love it!!**

Mexican Abalone
by Mr. Abaloneman (John Darby)

1 or 2 abalone, cleaned
1 large jar of salsa or homemade
1 bag of shredded Mozzarella or sharp cheese
1 avocado

Slice abalone vertically and pound to tenderize. Layer abalone, salsa, cheese and sliced avocado. Continue layering until all salsa, abalone, cheese and avocado are used. Place a layer of cheese on top. Bake at 350° for 30-45 minutes until you see a little bubbling in the glass pan. Serves 4 to 6 people with Spanish rice. **Delicious!**

Filet Taco Delight
by Filet

1 clean abalone
taco seasoning
tomato, chopped
lettuce, chopped
green onion, chopped
salsa
Monterey Jack cheese, grated

cooking oil
butter
corn tortilla

   Slice abalone into small pieces that can be ground through meat grinder. Fry corn tortillas in frying pan with cooking oil. Take out, fold and place on paper towel to dry off excess oil. Cook ground abalone same way as on taco seasoning packet. Fill up tortilla with abalone, tomato, onion, salsa, lettuce, and cheese. Serves 4 people. **Great for all kids.**

Abalone Burrito
by all deaf Mexican divers like me

1 clean abalone, slice and pound
1 can of green chiles, sliced
Monterey cheese, sliced
tomato, chopped
onion, chopped
salsa
flour tortilla

   Fry abalone steaks in frying pan with cooking oil. Take out steaks and cut to small pieces. Add abalone, chiles, tomato, cheese, onion and roll in hot flour tortillas. Serves 2-4 people. Can add salsa if you want.

Abalone Rellenos
by A. "Woody" Wood, Salt Point Ranger

2 to 4 abalone (depending on size)
2 to 4 cans whole green chiles
milk
flour
3 to 4 eggs
1 to 1-1/2 pounds cheese (jack or swiss)

Slice abalone crosswise or lengthwise and pound until tender. In a baking dish layer abalone, chiles (whole chiles) and cheese. Makes 2 to 4 layers of this. Mix 3 to 4 eggs, flour, salt and pepper in a batter with milk. It should be the consistency of pancake batter. Cover layers with batter. Bake 35 to 50 minutes at 350° until brown on top. **I ate his and I became more Mexican! Very good!**

Point Lobos Abalone Rellenos
by Ranger Jerry Loomis of Point Lobos State Reserve

Buy a big can of whole green chiles, the recipe is on the label (inside). Pound large, round pieces of abalone. Wrap the pieces around the chile. Use a tooth pick to secure the abalone to the chile. Dip the abalone into the batter described below and cook until the chile is golden brown. The abalone will be cooked when it is done. **Very good and real simple to cook!!!! Yo Te Quiero, Guardabosque Jerry!!!**

Relleno Batter
4 eggs, beaten
1-1/2 cups milk
1/4 cup flour
1/2 teaspoon salt
Combine eggs, milk, flour and salt until smooth.

Mexican Abalone Salad
by Abalone Lover's Cookbook

1 abalone
3 medium tomatoes, diced
1 medium onion, diced
1/4 cup catsup
1/4 cup olive oil
1 chopped green chili pepper

1 teaspoon minced oregano
1/2 teaspoon lime juice
1/2 teaspoon garlic powder
Salt and pepper to taste
Flour tortilla (optional)

Tenderize and steam abalone for 10 minutes, then cool and cut into small cubes. In a large bowl, mix abalone, tomatoes, and onions with catsup and olive oil. Add chili pepper, oregano, lime juice and seasonings and mix well. May serve with warm tortilla . Serves 4.

"Yo Te Quiero, Filet" Enchiladas

1 abalone, cleaned and ground
1-19 ounce can Enchilada sauce, divided sauce
1-4.5 ounce can chopped green chiles
3 cups (12 ounces) shredded Monterey Jack, divide cheese
1/2 cup chopped onion
8 corn tortillas
3/4 cup sour cream

In a medium skillet, combine abalone and 1/2 cup enchilada sauce, cook very quickly. Stir in green chiles and cheese (save 1 cup for top of enchiladas). In a small skillet, bring remaining enchilada sauce to a boil. Remove from heat. Dip each tortilla into heated sauce to soften. Spoon abalone mixture and 2 teaspoons of sour cream down center of each tortilla. Roll then place the tortillas seam-side down in 12x8 inch baking dish. Pour remaining heated sauce over top; sprinkle remaining cup of cheese on top. Bake about 20 minutes at 350°. Makes 4 servings with chopped onion sprinkled on top. **After trying this, you will say "Yo Te Quiero, Filet" ("I love you, Filet") again and again!!!!!!**

Captain Bob and Lorenzo with two five foot octopi, caught about 1,000 yards off Salt Point in 1992. Yes, they cooked and ate them. They were delicious!

Captain Bob's Abarito

This recipe I actually discovered myself after a lot of years in Mexico. It's a big hit. Prepare your abalone to your preference or as done in my abalone Italian. You can also use Krusteaz Tempura Batter instead of a crumb mixture.

1 abalone, sliced and pounded
2 packages. flour tortilla
1-16 ounce can whole ortega chilis
1 large package Monterey Jack cheese

Fry abalone and set aside. Cut chilis in half and set aside. Cut cheese in slices. Heat flour tortillas in a frying pan, place a slice of abalone, 1/2 of a whole ortega chili, slices of cheese, then roll or fold tortilla and rotate on pan until cheese has melted. "Serve and Enjoy"

Cinco de Mayo Abalone
by Tom Neth, North Coast State Parks Lifeguard

1 abalone (cut into steaks)
Eggs
Bread crumbs
Cheese
Can of green chiles
Jalapeño pepper

Cut abalone into steaks and pound. Dip into eggs and then bread crumbs. Place on a greased cookie sheet. Put a piece of cheese, a little piece of green chiles, and a piece of jalapeño pepper on each steak. Roll breaded abalone steak around cheese, chile and pepper. Secure with a toothpick if necessary. Bake at 350° for 15 minutes. **Got to be very delicious!!!!**

MISCELLANEOUS ABALONE RECIPES

Spaghetti in Italian Abalone Sauce
by Edward Whitt,
author of Cooking Abalone
and owner of Rohnert Park Dive Center

1 abalone, tenderized and cut into one into 1/2" cube
1/2 cup chopped onion
2 tablespoons olive oil
26 ounce jar of tomato and basil flavored pasta sauce
1 cup sliced zucchini
1/2 package spaghetti
Grated parmesan cheese to taste

In a large pot, cook onion and garlic in olive oil, until tender. Add jar of sauce and zucchini. Bring to a boil, reduce heat and simmer for ten minutes. Add abalone, cover and simmer for 8 to 10 minutes or until abalone is soft. In a separate pot cook the spaghetti. Break spaghetti in half before putting it in the pot. Drain and add sauce and parmesan, stir until spaghetti is fully coated. **This is very good to eat Try it and you will love it. Instead of pounding and cutting the abalone, you can grind it through a meat grinder.**

Garlic Abalone Noodles
by First Place winner 1994 Abalone Cookoff at Abalone Festival,
VanDamme State Park, Mendocino, CA

1 clean abalone
Garlic puree
Extra virgin olive oil
Chopped parsley
Cracked black pepper
Grated parmesan cheese

Abalone noodles:

This technique turns abalone into noodles which can be used as you would any other pasta. It eliminates the tenderizing process typically associated with making this tough mollusk (abalone) softer to be eaten. Having a meat slicer is needed to cut very thin slices. Partially freezing meat will give good results. Cut abalone, foot first, into 1/10" slices with very sharp knife cut the slices into thin strips about 1/10" wide. Blanch (to whiten or scald) the raw strips in a large pot of rapidly boiling water by dipping about 1 cup of strips at a time in a strainer for 10-15 seconds while stirring. Remove and immediately place strips into ice water and drain thoroughly. Abalone strips may be stored in refrigerator for up to 2 days.

Garlic puree:

Place 1 cup of peeled garlic cloves in a measuring cup and fill to 1 cup with extra virgin oil. Blend to a puree. Heat olive oil in a frying pan, 1/4 cup of oil per cup of noodles. Sauté about 1 teaspoon of garlic puree per cup of noodles for 10-20 seconds. Add abalone and stir to coat with garlic oil.

Remember noodles are already cooked and only need to be warmed. Overcooking can toughen them. Now add fresh cracked pepper and parsley to taste. Garnish with parmesan cheese and serve with French bread to soak up olive oil. **I was there and voted them first out of 40 recipes!!! It was very good although preparation takes a long time.**

Abalone Dip
by Celesta
a park aide who used to work at Fort Ross State Historic Park

1 abalone
Lime juice
2 small tomatoes, chopped
3 to 4 green onions, chopped
1 bell pepper, chopped
1 cucumber, sliced and chopped
1/2 cup Wesson oil

Slice and tenderize abalone very well. Cut into very small pieces. Put raw abalone in a bowl of lime juice and let stand for more than an hour. While abalone is in the bowl, chop all vegetables. Add lime juice to vegetables and mix fully. Let stand for half hour, stir often. Serve with chips. **Good snack!!!!**

Abalone Balls
by Steve Jackson
Owner of King's Sport & Tackle in Guerneville

2 fresh average-size abalone
1-1/4 cups graham cracker pieces
6 to 8 large ripe olives, pitted
1 medium-sized sweet onion
1 tablespoon prepared mustard
2 tablespoons dried parsley
2 eggs, beaten
2 tablespoons lemon juice
1/2 teaspoon salt
1/2 teaspoon seasoning salt
1/4 teaspoon black pepper
2 slices limp cooked bacon, crushed

Cut the abalone to edible portion, put the abalone, crackers, olives, and onion through a food grinder or chopper. Add the remaining ingredients, and mix thoroughly. Form into bite size balls and pan fry in an electric frying pan (about 300°) in small amounts of butter. Fry quickly while turning each piece (about 3 minutes) Do not overcook. Serve from chafing dish. Your guests won't be able to guess what they're eating, but they won't be able to stop at just one. Makes about 60 appetizers or 12 patties.

Note: Unsalted butter tends not to burn as quickly as salted when used for frying.

Don't forget your fishing license. Visit King's for your sport and fishing needs, a good filet knife, camping gear, to rent a kayak, or hear about the one that got away.

Abalone and Chanterelle Mushroom Salad
found on the Internet

1/4-1/2 pound chanterelle mushroom, fresh picked preferred
1 teaspoon minced shallots
1 tablespoon olive oil
1 tablespoon balsamic vinegar
1 clove garlic, crushed
2 tablespoons olive oil
salt and pepper
1 cup cherry tomatoes
chicken or fish stock
1 live abalone, 4-5 ounces, shucked, cleaned, and sliced 1/8" thick
   and pounded

      Preheat oven to 450 degrees. Clean and slice mushrooms. Toss with olive oil, garlic, salt and pepper. Spread on baking sheet; roast until tender. Pour stock into a skillet to a depth of 1/2", bring to simmer. Add abalone. Reduce heat; poach until tender, 30 to 45 seconds. Remove from liquid; let cool. Combine shallots with a pinch of salt and pepper and crush. Whisk in vinegar and oil. Adjust seasoning. Add abalone, mushrooms and tomatoes; toss to coat. **Delicious salad! I also add some mushrooms found in my park, or they can be purchased from local stores along the coast.**

Abalone Snack
by a camper at VanDamme State Park

1 abalone, sliced, pounded and fried
1 garlic, minced
about 5 shakes of oregano
about 6 shakes of parsley
about 1/4 coffee mug olive oil
1 spoon sugar
about 1/4 coffee mug chopped onion

Do what you usually do in fried abalone. Dry the fried abalone as much as you can, using a whole paper towel. Cut into bite-sized pieces. Put cooked abalone into a bowl of the above ingredients. Make sure all pieces are covered. Cover bowl with plastic wrap and put in a refrigerator overnight. Serve with a sauce like cocktail or Heinz 57 sauce. **Real good snack!!!**

Felix is holding a big mushroom, Boletus edilus, *about 4 pounds, found next to his backyuard, in 1992. He cooked for his friends his Famous Salt Point Omlette with mushroom, leftover abalone and vegetables.*

RECIPE INDEX

Recipe Index

BIBLIOGRAPHY

Cooking Abalone; A Collection of Recipes
By Edward Whitt
1996

The Abalone Lover's Cookbook
By Jeri Siegel and Michael Hill
1991

The Abalone Book
By Peter C. Howorth
1978

Mendocino County Coast Fishing & Diving Access Guide
By Rouvaishyara
Spring 1997

California Sport Fishing Regulations
State of California and Department of Fish and Game
Effective 3-1-98 though 2-28-2000, (unless otherwise noted herein)

California Abalone
State of California, Department of Fish and Game
Marine Resources Leaflets, No. 11
1986

All brochures of State Parks and Recreations
Salt Point State Park and Fort Ross State Historic Park

Independent Coast Observer
Gualala, California, Community Commitment newspaper since 1969